TRAINING DELIVERY SKILLS:
I
PREPARING THE TRAINING DELIVERY

Robert R. Carkhuff and Richard M. Pierce
With
John R. Cannon
Sharon G. Fisher
Ted W. Friel

Copyright © 1984 by
Human Resource Development Press, Inc.

22 Amherst Rd.
Amherst, Massachusetts 01002 (413) 253-3488

Bernice R. Carkhuff, Publisher

First Edition, First printing, January, 1984

Library of Congress Cataloging in Publication Data
International Standard Book Number 0-914234-73-0

Cover Art by Krawczyk
Cover Design by Tom Bellucci
Composition by The Magazine Group
Printing and Binding by Bookcrafters

Table of Contents

About the Authors

Robert R. Carkhuff, Ph.D., Chairman, Carkhuff Institute of Human Technology, Amherst, Massachusetts, is among the most-cited social scientists according to the Institute for Scientific Information. He is author of three of the most-referenced social science texts, including two volumes on *"Helping and Human Relations."* His latest books are *"Sources of Human Productivity"* and *"The Exemplary Performer in the Age of Productivity."*

Richard M. Pierce, Ph.D., Director, Human Resource Development, Human Technology, Inc., McLean, Virginia, has designed the implementation programs for more than 500 projects in the last 15 years. He is co-author of a forthcoming book on *"Performance Management Systems."*

John R. Cannon, Ph.D., Director, Management Systems, Human Technology, Inc., McLean, Virginia, has directed more than 600 projects in the last 12 years. He is co-author of a forthcoming book on *"The Art and Science of Consulting."*

Sharon G. Fisher, M.Ed., Director, Instructional Systems Design, Human Technology, Inc., McLean, Virginia, has designed hundreds of public and private sector instructional projects and products. She is recipient of the first *"Exemplar Award"* for her exemplary products in C.A.I. as well as print material.

Ted W. Friel, Ph.D., Director, Advanced Systems Design, Human Technology, Inc., McLean, Virginia, has done operations planning for more than 400 projects in the last 14 years. He is author of *"The Art of Developing a Career"* and co-author of a forthcoming book on *"Human Resource Planning."*

Foreword

In 1969, Carkhuff wrote the now landmark, *Helping and Human Relations*. Hailed as a classic in its time, it defined the operations of both counseling and training for the first time in human history.

In 1971, Carkhuff followed with the monumental *The Development of Human Resources*. Focusing upon education and training as the vehicles to human resource development, it operationalized the "human" goal in human resource development.

During the ensuing decade, Carkhuff and his associates developed the blueprint for education and the technologies for its teaching and learning skills. Written for teachers in 1981, *The Skilled Teacher* became a standard for trainers and developers in both the private and public sectors.

Now, based upon the extensive empirical evidence of hundreds of instructional design and productivity improvement efforts in business and government, Carkhuff and his associates bring us a package of volumes on *Instructional Systems Design* and *Training Delivery Skills*. I will focus upon the latter in my review.

I myself have been trained in the systems and skills of Carkhuff's "human technology." I have successfully utilized the models and technologies in my daily work efforts as a trainer, developer and manager of trainers and developers. These programs have produced dramatically positive results in terms of the performance of trainers, the productivity of training units and, above all, the productivity of the final recipients of these programs.

In considering training delivery skills, it is important to emphasize that our instructional design efforts are necessary but not sufficient conditions of our training deliveries. Our design efforts occur prior to contact with the trainees. How we implement the designs in interaction with the trainees dictates the effectiveness of our training efforts.

In this context, *Training Delivery Skills* teaches us the training delivery skills we need to make a successful training delivery. Volume I emphasizes the skills we need to prepare the training delivery. These preparation skills emphasize developing and organizing the training content, taking the trainees into consideration. They culminate in a training plan for managing the learning of the trainees.

Volume II teaches the critical skills for making a training delivery. These training delivery skills emphasize two sets of skills: 1) those involved in processing the trainees in terms of the requirements of the content; and 2) those involved in processing the content in terms of the trainees' experiences. That is, the trainers teach content! And they also teach trainees!

These critical training delivery skills are complemented by the training transfer skills necessary to insure transfer to the world of work. They are also supplemented by the training evaluation skills necessary to make assessments of our training efforts.

Training Delivery Skills is most valuable in a pre-service context where prospective trainers are being trained. It incorporates the very training skills in which the candidates are being trained: defining the training skill objectives; developing the skill content; developing the training delivery plan; and making the training delivery. It is also valuable for experienced trainers and instructional designers for purposes of programmatically reviewing or learning the training skills they were never taught. In this context, it may be fruitfully used in conjunction with the series on *Instructional Systems Design*.

To sum, *Training Delivery Skills* is a valuable text for all instructional personnel. It teaches training skills by a simple, step-by-step method. It emphasizes the all-too-often neglected training process between trainer and trainees. Our training effectiveness begins with our content and interpersonal processing skills. In the end, we are as effective as we are knowledgeable in our training content and skilled in our training delivery.

For delivering to us these training preparation and delivery skills, we owe Carkhuff and his associates a great debt of gratitude. For delivering to our clients our specialty contents, we owe our clients our best productivity efforts based upon those training delivery skills made available to us by Carkhuff and his associates.

Ed Feder, Manager
Training and Organizational Development
AMOCO Production Company
Standard Oil of Indiana

Preface

Recently, we had occasion to supervise the publication of a study on performance-based supervision. Conducted by a Fortune 100 corporation, it is presently the largest study of its kind. In the process of analyzing the data and the material, we became aware of the training standards of that corporation. Our lasting impression is one of several volumes of fold-out systems design and training technology specifications—surely a product of the Electronics Age, made in imitation of the engineering designs that launched the Age. The Electronics Age was systems-driven. Too often—especially in the human resource area—the system became a process that never really yielded a product.

These elaborated systems designs are, by themselves, inappropriate for the Information Age. The Information Age is driven by the productivity ethic of maximizing results outputs while minimizing resource inputs. This Information Age requires quick and powerful instructional designs by flexible and responsive *striking* forces. It requires the products of human processing.

In this context, we have written *Training Delivery Skills*, which emphasizes the training preparation and delivery skills necessary to produce and deliver training content. These volumes will enable trainers to design instructional intervention efficiently and effectively. With the aid of content experts, the skills presented herein will enable trainers to develop content fully and programmatically. In interaction with the trainees, these skills will enable the trainers to make their training deliveries readily and fluidly.

Training Delivery Skills is organized in modular form. After the introductory overview material, these volumes present skill modules organized around basic training principles. Above all, the modules emphasize the kinesthetic exercises that facilitate skill application and transfer and leave lasting images imprinted in our brains.

Training Delivery Skills is dedicated to instructional technologists and trainers in both the private and public sectors. As their jobs become increasingly more complex and time-limited, they will require the generic training skills presented in these volumes.

In creating these volumes on *Training Delivery Skills*, we are especially indebted to the following people: Dr. David H. Berenson for his understanding of teaching and training; James T. Chapados for his background materials; Bernice R. Carkhuff for her publishing responsibilities; Kathleen R. Bopp for her administrative assistance; and Janet Mendis for her editorial effort.

Education and training are the dominant sources of effect in human and information resource development in the Age of Information. Human and information resource development are the critical ingredients of economic productivity growth. In short, the future of a nation and its peoples, as well as a corporation or agency, lies in the hands of its education and training specialists. We dedicate these volumes to their productive efforts.

January, 1984   R.R.C. and R.M.P.
Washington, D.C.

I

INTRODUCTION AND OVERVIEW

I *he prepotent source of economic growth in the Age of Information is growth in the productivity component or organizational productivity. Improving individual performance is the principal source of improving organizational productivity. In turn, human and information resource development, i.e., "working smarter," is the source of improving individual performance. Finally, education and training are the sources of human and information resource development. Education and training may be defined by the following objectives: setting and achieving productivity goals; analyzing and performing the critical tasks needed to achieve the goals; defining and applying critical skills of the tasks; developing and acquiring the skills content; and making and receiving the training delivery.*

ECONOMIC GROWTH

↑

ORGANIZATIONAL PRODUCTIVITY

↑

INDIVIDUAL PERFORMANCE

↑

HUMAN AND INFORMATION RESOURCE DEVELOPMENT

↑

EDUCATION AND TRAINING

I

Training and Development in the Age of Information

We stand on the verge of an Information Revolution that challenges the very core of our humanity (Carkhuff, 1983a). For the first time in the 14-million-year history of humankind, humans must learn how to think or process this burgeoning information. At the same time, people are being challenged to develop not only their specialty substance or content but also the learning and teaching or training processes by which they develop their substance and disseminate it to others.

The critical activities of the Information Age are intellectual in nature. They emphasize the interdependent development of our intellectual selves (Carkhuff, 1983b). Indeed, interdependence may be defined by teaching and learning roles. We are all simultaneously both teachers and learners. We have both the power of our teaching roles and our substance and the power of our ability to learn new roles and new substance.

Synonyms for the Age of Information might be the Age of Human Processing or Human Productivity (Carkhuff, 1983a). In this new Age of Information, we must learn to process productively, i.e., to maximize our results outputs while minimizing our resource inputs. We all need to learn how to teach and train and learn productively. In this regard, we need to know the contextual dimensions of this new age in which we must function.

The Age of Information

The differences between the Industrial Age and the Information Age are both quantitative and qualitative. Yet they must be seen—as all human evolution—in a cumulative and developmental manner. Just as we continued to farm in the Industrial Age, so did we continue to manufacture in the Electronics Age. So also will we now continue to use computer hardware for mechanical processing in the Information Age.

The critical differences between the Industrial and Information Eras may be analyzed in terms of social, industrial, organizational and individual components (see Table 1-1). Clearly, the most critical resource shift is from capital to data or information (Naisbett, 1982). Relatedly, with the convergence of digital and telecommunication technologies, economics are pressured toward global rather than national emphases; governments move from central to decentralized units; politics move from partisan to issues-oriented.

Industrially, with the advent of data-based policy targeted specific goals for specific target populations, the great shift resultant from the information explosion is from manufacturing to services (Cox, 1982). Relatedly, marketing to satisfy customers displaces producing products to manipulate sales. Long-term investments in human and information resources replace short-term profitability. Finally, the sources of productivity emphasize reducing resource inputs while increasing results outputs.

With the abundance of information available to personnel at all levels, organizations, in turn, emphasize the people rather than the positions of leadership; interdependent rather than hierarchical relations; entrepreneurial initiative rather than managerial responsibilities, and person-to-person communication rather than role-to-role communication (Carkhuff, 1983a).

Similarly, with the changing data bases, individuals become generalists with multiple potential career specialties rather than specialists with single career possibilities.

Table 1-1
The Contextual Dimensions of the
Industrial and Information Eras

	CONTEXT	ERAS	
		Industrial	**Information**
Social	*Resources*	Capital	Data
	Economy	National	Global
	Government	Central	Decentralized
	Politics	Partisan	Issues
Industry	*Industry*	Manufacturing	Services
	Components	Production	Marketing
	Profitability	Short Term	Long Term
	Sources	Resource-Based	Productivity
Organizations	*Leadership*	Positions	People
	Organization	Hierarchical	Interdependent
	Responsibility	Managerial	Initiative
	Relations	Role-to-Role	Person-to-Person
Individuals	*Skills*	Specialists	Generalists
	Careers	Single	Multiple
	Motives	External	Internal
	Processing	Conditioning	Thinking

Individual motives move from external incentives to internal needs to achieve and actualize one's own individual as well as the organizational productivity potential. Most critical, individual processing shifts from the conditioned mentality of the Industrial Age to human processing or thinking in the Information Age (Carkhuff, 1983a).

The implications for education in general and training and development specifically are profound (Aspy, Aspy and Roebuck, 1984; McCune, 1984).

Sources of Economic Growth

Nowhere are these implications felt more heavily than in the economic sector. There the projected sources of growth in the Information Age establish human and informational resource development as the critical ingredients and education and training as the necessary vehicles (see Table 1-2).

Table 1-2
Sources of Projected Economic Growth

	% Growth Projected (1980–1990)	
	Moderate Growth	High Growth
Economic Growth (National Income)	**3.4**	**4.8**
Factor Input Sources:	1.8	2.2
Human Resources	(1.3)	(1.4)
Capital Resources	(0.5)	(0.8)
Organizational Productivity Sources:	1.6	2.6
Information Sources	(0.9)	(1.3)
Human Resources	(1.0)	(1.1)
Individual Performance Sources:	1.0	1.1
Education and Training	(0.8)	(0.9)
Health	(0.1)	(0.1)
Work Force Composition	(0.1)	(0.1)

As can be seen, economic prognosticators calculate the percent of growth in national income in the 3.4% to 4.8% range for the 1980's (Carnavale, 1983; Denison, 1979; Grayson, 1980; Kendrick, 1979). Of these projections of economic growth, about 50% are a function of human and capital resource inputs and about 50% a function of organizational productivity components. (There is some trend for the influence of the productivity factors to rise as the economic growth projections are raised.)

Of the factor input sources of economic growth, somewhere around two-thirds are accounted for by human resources with the remaining one-third accounted for by capital resources. In other words, human resources play a dominant role in accounting for the influence of inputs upon economic growth.

The influences upon the organizational productivity sources, in turn, are about equally divided between the information and human resources. (There is some trend for the influence of information to rise as the projections of economic growth are raised.) In general, human and information resource development account for the great majority of the effects of organizational productivity growth. (There are some depressor factors that contribute negatively to economic growth.) The dominance of these sources represents a dramatic transformation from the earlier dominance of capital, natural and even land resources.

Viewing human and information resource development in a cyclical interaction with each other is most helpful. Improving the quality of personnel improves the quality of advancements in knowledge which, in turn, serves to further elevate human resource development. When seen in interaction with each other, human and information resource development define the theme of "working smarter" that dominates the Information Age and promises to produce many times more than the theme of "working harder" that dominated the Industrial Era.

It is critical to understand that by far the greatest source of human resource development is education and training. In general, education and training account for around 80% of the variance in human resource development, with health making a critical but not dominant contribution. (The combination of the work force, i.e., age, sex and other demographics, is projected to make increasingly positive yet relatively minimal contributions.)

Good sense dictates that education and training play an increasingly dominant role in the Age of Information. With the spiraling requirements for processing information, education and training converge upon the sources of effectiveness in human and information resource development: the development and dissemination of substantive advancements in skills and knowledge; and the refinement of the teaching and learning processes facilitating the individual development of these skills and knowledge.

In short, education and training are the critical sources of the improved processing that contributes to the development of human and informational resources. In turn, human and informational resource development are the effective ingredients in productivity specifically and all economic growth generally.

Training and Development

The implications for training and development in both the private and public sectors are, indeed, quite profound. Already, industry and government are spending amounts ranging above $30 billion on training and development. Depending upon how progressively public education integrates its effort with a productivity ethic, this amount could easily range upward toward $50 billion in the near future.

In order to develop a more productive perspective of

training and development, we may analyze this area in the same manner that we analyze any business or government organization (Table 1-3). As can be seen, the differences between the components, functions and processes of the Industrial and Information Ages are vast (Carkhuff, 1983a).

Components
Clearly, the resource components shift from an emphasis upon capital to an emphasis upon information. Just like all other units, training and development sections are being asked to become more productive, i.e., to do more with

Table 1-3
Training and Development

	DIMENSIONS	ERAS	
		Industrial	Information

Components	Resources
	Production
	Marketing and
	  Distribution
		Capital-Based
		Industry-Centered
		Internal
			Information-Based
			Community Centered
			Internal and
			  External

Functions	Policy Management Supervision Delivery	Corporate Board Director Manager Trainer	Comunity-Oriented Systems Designer Intervention Designer Instructional Designer

Processes	Input
	Output
	Processes
	Feedback
		Trainees
		Specific Skills
		S → R Conditioning
		Applications
			Trainees (Learners)
			General Processing
			  Skills
			Human & Computer
			  Processing
			Transfers & Productiv-
			  ity Achievements

less. Indeed, information is seen as being universally related to the investment of other resources.

In terms of production and marketing, there is a necessary shift from being centered around local business operations to expanding to incorporate community, regional, national and even international perspectives. Again, the level of expansion depends upon the reciprocity of the relationship between public education and private training.

Relatedly, marketing and distribution move from an internal-industry emphasis to both internal and external emphases. Because of its expanding mission, training and development must market and distribute its products and services externally in relation to the community-at-large as well as internally for the immediate benefit of one or more units.

Functions

The functions of the traditional hierarchy will also change dramatically. Corporate boards as well as public policy-making bodies will be increasingly oriented toward the community-at-large and increasingly attuned to the constantly changing data bases. This new orientation means that the policy-makers must have programmatic policy-making skills: they must be able to generate, analyze, synthesize, project and interpret data in order to define their missions in terms of accurate goals and appropriate target populations. They must be able to engage in strategic decision-making and planning concerning the abilities of the resource, production, marketing and distributing components to achieve their missions (Carkhuff, 1983a).

In turn, the directors of industrial relations, personnel or HRD (Human Resource Development) must be equipped with the skills of model builders and systems designers: they must be able to design productivity systems to achieve changing missions based upon the constantly changing data inputs. These productivity designs must emphasize the components, functions and processes of individual human performance as well as organizational productivity (Carkhuff, 1983a).

The managers or supervisors of training and development or educational services must have the skills of intervention design: they must be equipped with the skills to make the interventions necessary to develop the productivity systems designed by the directors and their staffs. These interventions must emphasize establishing productivity goals in terms of results outputs and resource inputs as well as analyzing contextual tasks to define quantitative and qualitative performance indices (Carkhuff, 1983a; Carkhuff, Fisher, Cannon, Friel, and Pierce, 1984).

Finally, the training and development and evaluation personnel must have fully developed the skills of instructional system design: they must be able to operationally define any skill objective and develop a skill content to achieve that objective. They must be able to develop a training delivery plan and to implement that delivery in such a facilitative manner as to insure the reception of that training content by the recipients.

These functions must be discharged interdependently within training and development just as they are within an industry or a government agency: all personnel at all levels of policy, management, supervision and delivery must be in constant and constructive revolution with the missions they receive. Because the data are constantly changing and because those most intimate with the data know them best, each individual serves the larger corporate or agency mission by taking appropriate data-based initiatives to fulfill that mission.

Processes
The changes in the processes are just as profound. In terms

of inputs, it is acceptable to continue to think of recipients of training as trainees. However, it is important to emphasize that they are now redefined as active learners, not simply passive recipients of responses. Indeed, the processes must be designed to facilitate the active learning.

Output is redefined to emphasize in learner-products a core or cluster of generic processing skills. A number of specific skill clusters will rotate around this core as the personnel accumulate new data and learn new skills.

Whereas Stimulus → Response conditioning dominated the training processes during the Industrial Age, human and computer processing now dominate during the Information Age. In this context, mechanical processing of all kinds is driven by human processing. The human is the source of the dramatic changes in the Information Age, and the computer and other mechanical appendages are critical tools for implementing human designs for human benefits.

In this regard, whereas feedback on skill acquisition and application was emphasized in the Industrial Era, task transfers and productivity achievements now dominate. This means that the trainee-learners need to perform the tasks that achieve the goals that were specified in the first place. The basic evaluation question for all learning is whether or not the trainee-learners achieved the productivity goals of the training.

In summary, the components of training and development emphasize extensive, if not universal, data bases. The functions emphasize systematically designed and implemented data-based missions. The processes emphasize incremental training-learning wherein both trainers and trainee-learners process incrementally more than the training stimulus experience is calculated to elicit.

The transition to Information Age ingredients will not be a smooth one. We are already in a period of fragmentation, as our social, economic, political and educational institutions lag behind the requirements imposed by the new age. Clearly, many of the necessary changes will not come easily. For example, if personnel follow the productivity principle and eliminate their own jobs, what kind of place will there be for them in that particular private or public context? Clearly a profound accompanying need exists for changing the values of justice that accompany the values of productivity, i.e., there must be a change in the cultural values and milieu in which the changes take place.

A Training Overview

In Book I, we are going to concentrate upon preparing the training delivery beginning with the definition of training skill objectives. In Book II, we are going to emphasize making the training delivery beginning with using our training delivery skills to implement our delivery plan.

In these volumes, we are going to concentrate upon developing and delivering the training content and facilitating the trainees' reception of the content. We will begin with the training skills objectives and the skills content. These define the initial stations of the instructional system design skills that will define training skills in the Age of Information. Our training skills objective is for our trainees to become productive trainers:

The instructional trainers will develop and implement their training delivery to their trainees by learning training preparation and training delivery skills, that are to be used in formal and informal training situations, at levels that facilitate trainee achievement.

This training objective, in turn, is based upon our learnings concerning the principles of training effectiveness.

We may summarize these learnings about training effectiveness in the form of training principles. These training and learning principles constitute the core of the chapters that follow. The first set of training principles emphasizes the trainer's preparation of the content for the trainees (Book 1):

1. In preparing the content for training, productive trainers define the objectives in terms of the operations needed to achieve them: *all productive content culminates in skill objectives.*

2. In developing the content, productive trainers develop the atomistic steps necessary to achieve the skill objectives: *all productive content moves programmatically to the skill objectives.*

3. In developing the content, productive trainers develop the knowledge necessary to support achieving the skill objectives: *all productive content requires supportive knowledge.*

4. In organizing the content, productive trainers develop sequencing that is responsive to the trainees' naturalistic learning patterns: *all productive content is organized around the skill application.*

5. In developing the training methods, productive trainers present the skills content through a variety of sensory modalities, especially kinesthetic: *all productive training methods emphasize a variety of sensory modalities.*

6. In developing their delivery plans, productive trainers organize the content and the training methods around the content: *all productive delivery plans emphasize an integration of content and methods.*

The second set of training principles emphasizes the trainer's delivery of the content to the trainees (Book II):

7. In implementing their delivery plans, productive trainers emphasize managing training: *all productive delivery plans emphasize trainee management.*

8. In involving the trainees in training, productive trainers develop training experiences which incorporate the process orientation, style, creativity, structural and functional properties of training: *all productive training involves the naturalistic patterns found in experiential exploration, personalized understanding, and behavioral action.*

9. In delivering the skills content, productive trainers make moment-to-moment diagnoses of the trainees' needs in terms of the skills content and develop the resultant programming to meet these needs: *all productive training delivery is broken down into atomistic steps based upon diagnoses of the trainees' functioning on the skills content.*

10. In facilitating the training delivery, productive trainers individualize programs in terms of the trainees' internal frames of reference: *all productive training begins with the trainees' frames of reference.*

11. In relating the content to the trainees' contexts, productive trainers use transfer skills to insure the transfer of the skills to real-life functioning: *all productive training culminates in transfer learning.*

12. In completing the training delivery, productive trainers use evaluation skills to evaluate the training process and outcome: *all productive training is evaluated by systematic evaluation skills.*

The skills training chapters are presented in modular form. They are broken down into atomistic learning steps that should provide a model for training modules: an entry training experience; a review of the relevant literature defining the principles involved; an index of skill performance; an overview of skill dimensions; the skill steps and supportive knowledge involved; application and transfer exercises;

and a summary of the skills. The skills training is broken down page-by-page to facilitate learning.

References

Aspy, D.N., Aspy, C.B. and Roebuck, F.N. *The Third Century in American Education.* Amherst, Mass.: Human Resource Development Press, 1984.

Carkhuff, R.R. *Sources of Human Productivity.* Amherst, Mass.: Human Resource Development Press, 1983.(a)

Carkhuff, R.R. *Interpersonal Skills and Human Productivity.* Amherst, Mass.: Human Resource Development Press, 1983.(b)

Carkhuff, R.R., Fisher, S.G., Cannon, J.R., Friel, T.W. and Pierce, R.M. *Instructional Systems Design, Volumes I and II.* Amherst, Mass.: Human Resource Development Press, 1984.

Carnavale, A. *Human Capital.* Washington, D.C.: American Society for Training and Development, 1983.

Cox, A. *The Cox Report on the American Corporation.* New York: Cox, 1982.

Denison, E. *Accounting for Slower Economic Growth.* Washington, D.C.: Brookings Institution, 1979.

Grayson, C.J. *The U.S. Economy and Productivity.* Washington, D.C.: Joint Economic Committee, 1980.

Kendrick, J. *Productivity Trends and the Recent Slowdown.* Washington, D.C.: American Enterprise Institute, 1979.

McCune, S. "Reframing Education in the Age of Information." Chapter 6 in Aspy, D.N., Aspy, C.B. and Roebuck, F.N. (Eds.), *The Third Century in American Education.* Amherst, Mass.: Human Resource Development Press, 1984.

Naisbett, J. *Megatrends.* New York: Warner, 1982.

DESIGNING SYSTEMATIC INTERVENTIONS

Intervention design is a means by which goals are transformed into real achievements. Intervention emphasizes systematically intervening to build in success every step of the way to achieving our goals. Consulting interventions emphasize expanding strategies or models of change. Training interventions emphasize delivering skills to the implementers of the resultant programs. Systematic interventions emphasize the systematic transformation of missions into their achievement through planning, implementation and evaluation.

PLANNING ACHIEVEMENT

Mission Mission

Goals Goals

Tasks Tasks

Skills Skills

Steps Steps

2

Designing Consulting Systems: An Overview

Most instructional design personnel do not begin with a consulting intervention. They are usually not involved with policy-makers or high-level decision-makers. Policy-makers or their representatives such as Chief Executive Officers (C.E.O.'s) are the personnel that initiate a consulting intervention design. Increasingly, with the information demands of the Information Age, these executive officers will have either external or internal consultants to guide them through the consulting intervention. The purpose of the consulting intervention is to refine the mission of the executive officers based upon the best available data. The mission is defined by developing strategic goals, making strategic decisions and developing strategic plans for implementing the mission. This chapter will overview consulting system design (Carkhuff, 1983, 1984; Carkhuff, Fisher, Cannon, Friel and Pierce, 1984).

The consulting intervention is initiated when the

consultants work with the executive officers to formulate productivity missions. These missions are simply statements of specific goals for different populations. The goals may be loosely defined initially. The purpose of the consulting intervention is to refine these goals more precisely. The target populations may be external or internal. External target populations, such as customers, have implications for internal populations, such as management. The productivity goals are usually stated in terms of results outputs and/or resource inputs:

$$\text{PRODUCTIVITY} = \frac{\text{RESULTS OUTPUTS}}{\text{RESOURCE INPUTS}}$$

In the ideal, productivity goals attempt to improve results outputs while reducing resource inputs.

CONSULTANT

Mission

Formulating Productivity Missions

For example, with external populations, the results improvement goals may range as follows:

Using new and more powerful resources
Producing new and more profitable products
Segmenting new and more profitable markets
Developing universal methods of distribution

Similarly, with external populations, the resource reduction goals may vary as follows:

Reducing old and more expensive resources
Reducing old and unprofitable products
Reducing old and unprofitable markets
Reducing archaic distribution methods

Formulating External Population Goals

With internal populations, the results improvement goals may vary over the following themes:

Increasing critical personnel, information and capital resources
Increasing production capacity
Increasing marketing share
Increasing distribution facility

Similarly, with internal populations, the resource reduction goals may range as follows:

Reducing capital expenditures in materials, methods, equipment, time, energy and space
Reducing production expenditures
Reducing marketing expenditures
Reducing distribution expenditures

Formulating Internal Population Goals

These productivity missions dictate an analysis of strategic components. Strategic components are the components that we require to achieve our missions. Usually, productivity missions emphasize the following components:

Resource Component
Production Component
Marketing Component
Distribution Component

We analyze the components in order to refine the goals for any one or more of the critical components necessary to achieve our mission.

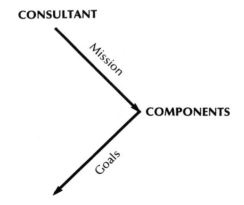

Analyzing Strategic Components

For example, we may state the strategic goals within any one of the strategic components as follows:

$$\text{RESOURCE GOALS} = \frac{\text{Improving resource capacity } (+20\%)}{\text{Reducing resource expenditures } (-10\%)}$$

$$\text{PRODUCTION GOALS} = \frac{\text{Improving production capacity } (+5\%)}{\text{Maintaining production expenditures}}$$

$$\text{MARKETING GOALS} = \frac{\text{Maintaining market share}}{\text{Reducing marketing expenditures } (-25\%)}$$

$$\text{DISTRIBUTION GOALS} = \frac{\text{Maintaining delivery outputs}}{\text{Maintaining distribution expenditures}}$$

As can be seen, strategic goals usually emphasize improving results outputs and/or reducing resource inputs. Often it is necessary to make resource expenditures, such as investments in training, in order to increase results outputs. Then we are interested in the Return-on-Investment (R.O.I.). The R.O.I. is simply a ratio of the increments in results benefits brought about by the added resource investments:

$$\text{R.O.I.} = \frac{\text{Results increments}}{\text{Added resource expenditures}}$$

Establishing Strategic Goals

   With the strategic goals for our critical components in hand, we may set about to make strategic decisions. Strategic decisions enable us to determine the most cost-beneficial courses of action for achieving our goals. We may use the values of the executive officers embedded in the mission to discriminate the most productive or preferred course or courses of action to achieve the goal. Again, the preferred course of action will be the one that maximizes the probability of achieving the strategic goals.

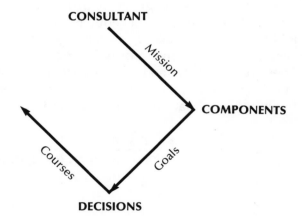

Making Strategic Decisions

For example, in attempting to achieve a strategic personnel goal in the resource component, we may consider variations of the following basic strategies:

I. *Increase Capacity* — increase personnel by hiring
II. *Acquire Capacity* — purchase or subcontract capacity
III. *Develop Capacity* — train existing personnel

In each of these instances, we would apply our productivity values to making the most cost-beneficial decisions. The preferred strategic course of action would be that which satisfied our values best.

Selecting Strategic Courses of Action

Armed with the preferred course or courses of action, we may now engage in strategic planning. Strategic planning involves the design of the plans to implement the preferred courses of action that enable us to achieve the appropriate goals of our productivity mission. Strategic plans are detailed to the task level. The tasks define the responsibilities or duties of critical units and performers.

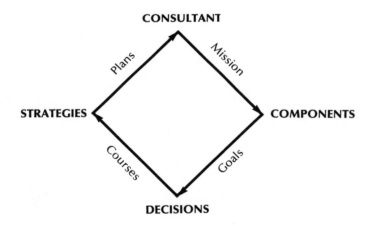

Engaging in Strategic Planning

For example, having chosen some variation of the resource development course of action, we may now develop strategic plans for making training and other related interventions within the resource component. As can be seen, we have now defined the tasks of the training intervention.

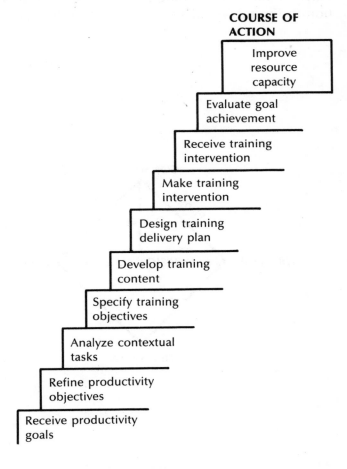

COURSE OF ACTION

Improve resource capacity

Evaluate goal achievement

Receive training intervention

Make training intervention

Design training delivery plan

Develop training content

Specify training objectives

Analyze contextual tasks

Refine productivity objectives

Receive productivity goals

Developing Strategic Plans

We may now deliver our strategic plans to the decision-makers who are usually the managers of the various components. The strategic plans emphasizing task responsibilities are submitted to these decision-makers for their processing. They may modify the results goals in relation to the resource expenditures. Similarly, the decision-makers may fine-tune the training resource expenditures in relation to the projected performance increments.

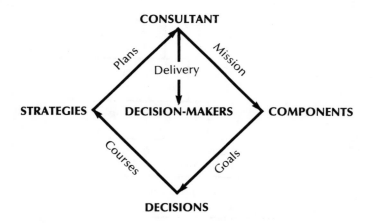

Making the Strategic Delivery

In other words, the consultants are presenting a strategic planning model for achieving the original productivity mission. The decision-makers have an opportunity to process and refine the model. In so presenting, the consultants are initiating a feedback loop for assessing the effects of the strategic planning.

Processing the Strategic Model

The feedback loop allows us to evaluate the effects of our presentation of the strategic planning model. We can determine whether the decision-makers: 1) can receive our presentation; 2) can acquire an understanding of the strategic plans; 3) can apply those plans to implement strategic courses of action; 4) can transfer the courses to the goals of their components; and 5) can achieve the original productivity mission.

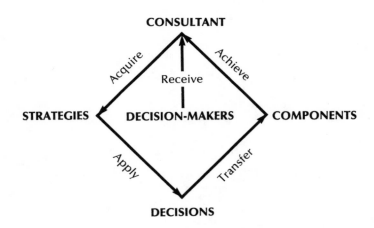

Evaluating Consulting Achievements

The net effect of the evaluation is to refine the original productivity mission of the executive officers. These refinements are manifested in more precise definitions of goals for the critical component areas. Thus, for example, the training intervention plan for the development courses of action in the resource component may be refined in terms of the following: improvement, reduction and maintenance goals for both results outputs and the resource inputs with the targeted population.

TARGET POPULATIONS

	RESULTS OUTPUTS	RESOURCE INPUTS
GOALS		
Improving	_____	_____
Reducing	_____	_____
Maintaining	_____	_____

Refining Productivity Mission

Again, most instructional design personnel do not begin with the consulting intervention. Yet they are recipients of the refined goals that are a product of that intervention. In that context, it is important that instructional design personnel understand the source of the productivity goals they receive. That way they can initiate their own instructional intervention finely attuned to the original productivity mission. In the end, the intentions of the framers of that mission and the processing of the data by the implementers of that mission will account for its achievement.

References

Carkhuff, R.R. *Sources of Human Productivity*. Amherst, Mass.: Human Resource Development Press, 1983.

Carkhuff, R.R. *Consulting System Design*. Amherst, Mass.: Carkhuff Institute of Human Technology, 1984.

Carkhuff, R.R., Fisher, S.G., Cannon, J.R., Friel, T.W. and Pierce, R.M. *Instructional Systems Design*, Volumes I and II. Amherst, Mass.: Human Resource Development Press, 1984.

3

Designing Instructional Systems: An Overview

Most of us first encountered instructional design in the teaching curricula we experienced in school. Typically, the teacher had a yearly content which he or she broke out in terms of units, topics, tasks and skills. Twenty years ago, instructional systems in business and industry were constructed in much the same manner as a good math or science or vocational education program. Now we are being asked to train in anything from learning-to-learn skills to computer processing. The tasks have become multifaceted and the timeliness have become telescoped. Increasingly, we are being asked to design entire training systems and technologies within a matter of months or even weeks. No longer can we afford the plateaus of "yearly content." Just as the industries that will survive and grow in the Information Age, training and development specialists and their units must become flexible and responsible striking forces. Indeed, the agencies and industries will be productive to the degree their training arms are responsive to their ever-changing needs.

Training design or instructional systems design is best conceived of as part of a larger system of interventions that we may label productivity system design. In its most productive context, instructional design is preceded by consulting design which delivers the refined productivity goals to the instructional technologist or trainer. These goals drive the instructional system.

The training skill objective of this book is for the *instructional trainees to be able to prepare the training delivery. They will do so by developing the training content and delivery plan. they will do so under formal and informal work conditions. They will do so at levels that insure trainee skill acquisition, application and transfer.*

Before you learn to identify and perform the skills of training design, you may want an index of your present level of understanding. Take some time to outline the critical tasks of training design.

_____

_____

_____

Indexing Training Design Skills

You did well if you emphasized the activities needed to achieve training skill objectives: defining the training skill objectives; developing the skills content; developing a delivery plan; making the training delivery; and evaluating the training delivery. Each of these training design tasks, in turn, may be broken down into different development and delivery skills as follows:

Defining training skill objectives—defining operations of skill objectives
Developing skills content—developing skill steps and knowledge
Developing delivery plan—organizing content and delivery methods
Making the training delivery—using training delivery and transfer skills
Evaluating the delivery—assessing training process and outcome

Again, these are all training design tasks that are part of the larger productivity and intervention design systems.

Overviewing Training Design Skills

Establishing Productivity Goals

Instructional systems design begins and ends with productivity goals. Ideally, the productivity goals are forwarded from systematic consulting interventions. The productivity goals define the goals for the components or units within the components. They emphasize the relationship between results outputs (RO) and resource inputs (RI). These goals drive the entire instructional system. They may emphasize effectiveness or improvement of results outputs $\left(\frac{RO+}{RI}\right)$. They may also improve efficiency or reduce resource inputs $\left(\frac{RO}{RI-}\right)$. An ideal productivity goal emphasizes effectiveness and efficiency simultaneously $\left(\frac{RO+}{RI-}\right)$.

TRAINER

Goals

Establishing Productivity Goals

Individualized unit goals are derived from these productivity goals. Unit goals are defined for those key result areas that impact the productivity goals. For example, when trying to increase the personnel capacity, the training and development section may be a key result area in the resource component. Thus, a productivity goal for increasing personnel capacity by 20% while maintaining the current training resource expenditures may be translated directly to the training unit goal:

$$\text{UNIT PRODUCTIVITY GOAL} = \frac{\text{Personnel Capacity } (+20\%)}{\text{Training Expenditures}}$$

Individualizing Goals for Key Result Areas

In turn, the individualized unit goals may be measured. Both inputs and outputs may be measured by quantitative and/or qualitative measures. Quantitative measures emphasize volume, rate and timeliness.

Quantitative Measures:
    Volume: How much?
      Rate: How many per unit of time?
  Timeliness: On time?

In turn, qualitative measures emphasize accuracy, functionality and initiative.

Qualitative Measures:
    Accuracy: How well done?
  Functionality: Does it work?
    Initiative: New approaches?

Measuring Goals

For example, we may measure the inputs and outputs of training by any one or more of the following measures:

Quantitative Measures:
　　　Volume: How many personnel trained?
　　　Rate: How many personnel trained per week?
　Timeliness: How many personnel ready on time?

Qualitative Measures:
　　Accuracy: How skilled are personnel?
Functionality: How effective in task performance?
　Initiative: What new productive training approach?

The individualized unit productivity goals become the goals of the intervention (Carkhuff, 1983, 1984; Carkhuff, Fisher, Cannon, Friel, and Pierce, 1984).

Establishing Productivity Goals

Analyzing Contextual Tasks

Armed with the individualized unit goals, the trainer may engage in an analysis of the contextual tasks needed to achieve the goals. Contextual task analysis addresses the requirement of the context. The individuals must perform context-specific tasks in order to achieve the unit's goals. The contextual task analysis emphasizes the process tasks by which inputs are transformed into outputs. Contextual task performance is measured by a comparison of outputs to inputs.

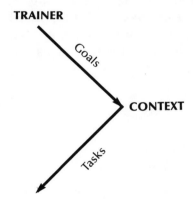

Analyzing Contextual Tasks

For example, work flow analyses may be conducted within delivery or production tasks.

Delivery Tasks:
Preparing
Performing
Assessing

Thus, preparation tasks such as receiving, assembling and organizing materials and scheduling activities may be analyzed. Also, performing tasks such as planning and implementing the skills involved might be emphasized. Finally, assessing tasks such as checking, documenting and quality controlling might be included. In a similar manner, planning, organizing, directing, controlling and appraising supervisory tasks could be analyzed. Likewise, planning, coordinating, prioritizing, implementing, monitoring and reviewing management tasks could be analyzed.

Analyzing Process Tasks

In addition, we may analyze the barriers to the performance of these process tasks. There are three primary sources of these barriers: the personnel, themselves; the environment or organization; and information. There are physical, emotional and intellectual dimensions to each of these sources. An analysis of these barriers will yield the tasks that enable personnel to perform the process tasks needed to achieve the unit objective (Carkhuff, 1983, 1984; Carkhuff, Fisher, Cannon, Friel, and Pierce, 1984; Gilbert, 1978).

BARRIER DIMENSIONS

BARRIER SOURCES

	Physical	**Emotional**	**Intellectual**
Personnel	Capacity?	Motives?	Skills?
Environment	Resources?	Incentives?	Procedures?
Information	Tasks?	Mission?	Flow?

Analyzing Enabling Tasks

Initiating the Training Delivery

The level at which most trainers and developers enter the instructional design system is defining training objectives. Usually, someone else has determined the productivity goals and conducted the contextual task analyses. The goals transmitted to the trainers and developers is to develop a training program to improve functioning in inspecting or disseminating or communicating or MBO (Management by Objectives). It is at this point that the trainers and developers are consulted to initiate the training delivery tasks: define training objectives; develop training skills content; develop training delivery plan; make the training delivery; and evaluate the training delivery.

Initiating Training Delivery

Instructional System Design

Once the contextual tasks have been analyzed, the tasks may be broken down into skills. Ideally, skills will comprise the objectives of training. Skills emphasize the need of the individual to perform the tasks. Suppose, for example, we chose to define the analyzing and diagnosing skills of inspection tasks. Or we might define the work content, delivery plan, interpersonal and delivery skills of the pre-supervision planning tasks. Or we might define the MBO or PERT or PPBS skills of management planning tasks. Specifying and defining the training objectives is the topic of Chapter 4 in Book I of *Training Delivery Skills*.

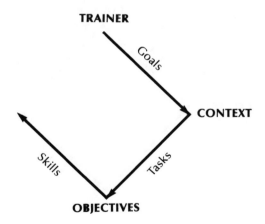

Defining Training Objectives

With the training objectives specified and defined, we may now proceed to develop the training skills content. The skills content emphasizes the skills steps and supportive knowledge needed to achieve the training objectives. Thus we might, for example, develop the skills steps for analyzing the components of an inspection task. Or we might develop the skills steps for developing the work assignments at the supervisory level. Or we might develop the skills steps for defining the mission for a planning skill objective at the management level. Developing the skills content is the topic of both Chapters 5 and 6 in Book I of *Training Delivery Skills.*

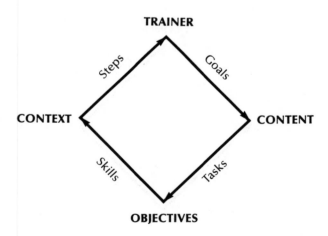

Developing Skills Content

With the skills content in hand, we must now develop a training delivery plan. A training delivery plan emphasizes both organizing the content and developing the training methods. There are many ways to deliver the skills content. All productive delivery plans emphasize the trainees exercising the skill steps of the training skills content. Developing a delivery plan is the topic of Chapters 7, 8 and 9 in Book I of *Training Delivery Skills*.

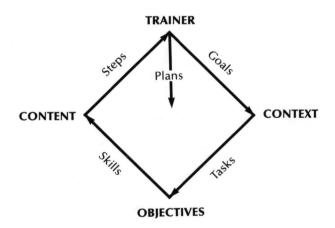

Developing the Delivery Plan

Next we must make the training delivery. Making the training delivery involves implementing the delivery plan. All productive training deliveries emphasize both the training content (content processing skills) and the trainees' experience of the content (interpersonal skills). In short, it is the trainer's task to relate the trainees' experience to the training content. Making the training delivery is the topic of Chapters 2 through 4 in Book II of *Training Delivery Skills.*

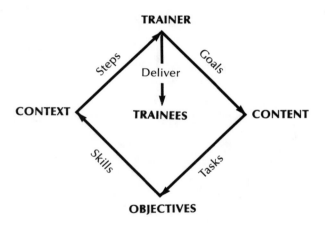

Making the Training Delivery

Finally, having made the training delivery, we must now address evaluating it. Evaluating the training delivery emphasizes going counter-clockwise around the "Productivity Diamond": assessing the trainees' level of process movement in receiving the delivery; assessing the trainees' level of acquisition of the skills content; assessing the trainees' level of application to the training objectives; assessing the trainees' level of transfer of skills to the contextual tasks; and assessing the trainees' level of goal achievement. Ultimately, we must determine whether or not the trainees have achieved our original productivity goals. If not, we can trace back over the other levels of process and outcome to determine sources of effect. Evaluating the training delivery is the topic of Chapter 5 in Book II of *Training Delivery Skills*.

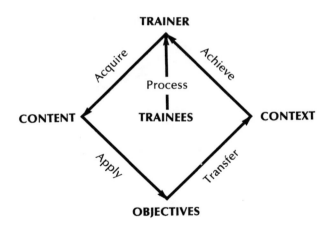

Evaluating the Training Delivery

In summary, for most training and development personnel, instructional design begins with the assignment of the training goal resultant from a front-end analysis. It remains for trainers to define the training objectives; develop the training content; and plan, make and evaluate the training delivery. Increasingly, instructional design is driven by productivity goals that determine the contextual tasks to be analyzed. Relating instructional design and training delivery to productivity goal achievement is a critical step in instructional technology in the Age of Information. The "Productivity Diamond" is our guide to all critical stations in productivity improvement.

References

Carkhuff, R.R. *Sources of Human Productivity*. Amherst, Mass.: Human Resource Development Press, 1983.

Carkhuff, R.R. *Consulting System Design*. Amherst, Mass.: Carkhuff Institute of Human Technology, 1984.

Carkhuff, R.R., Fisher, S.G., Cannon, J.R., Friel, T.W. and Pierce, R.M. *Instructional System Design, Volumes I and II*. Amherst, Mass.: Human Resource Development Press, 1984.

Gilbert, T.F. *Praxeonomy: A Scientific Approach to Identifying Training Needs*. Ann Arbor, Mich.: University of Michigan Graduate School of Business, 1978.

III

DEVELOPING THE TRAINING CONTENT

We may think of the training content much as we do
management-by-objectives. In consulting, we first
develop our productivity goals. We then analyze the tasks
needed to achieve the goals. In developing the training content, we first define the training skills objectives. Then we
break out our objectives in terms of skills steps and the supportive knowledge needed to perform them.

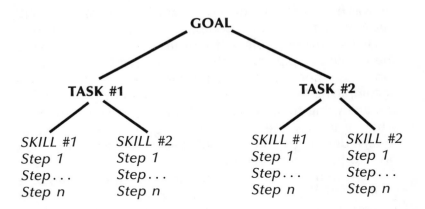

4

Defining Training Objectives

During the Spanish American War, Frederick W. Taylor was made manager of the Bethlehem Steel Company. He was hired for one purpose, to apply his ideas of "Scientific Management" to the company to try to increase its productivity. One example of his results was that he increased the loading of pig iron onto railroad cars from 12½ long tons a day per man to 47½ long tons a day per man. He accomplished this by observing the tasks the men had to do, analyzing their separate operations, relating them to what he already knew about the fatigue factor of men and finally, defining skill objectives before he taught the men how to perform the tasks.

Dr. John Hubolt made possible the Apollo Mission's goal—putting a person on the moon—by identifying a set of operations using several different space vehicles, thus making one of humankind's greatest dreams a reality. We have all had experiences in our lives of being told, and then trying, to do a job without knowing what the goals are or, for that matter, when they have been achieved. This is not an unusual phenomenon for workers. Indeed, trainers, themselves, are also not always precise in defining their training objectives. Consequently, the trainees or employees may not really know how to achieve them.

Review and Overview

Worker productivity is contingent upon how well the work tasks are defined. The operations needed to implement a task can be defined in terms of both the specific work tasks leading to the objective and the generic skills that underlie the specific work tasks (French, 1957; Kearny, 1953; Mager, 1962, 1968, 1972; Odiorne, 1965; Pipe, 1975). Many instructional design personnel continue to design instructional systems to accomplish work tasks. Increasing numbers attempt to deal with the behavioral activities or skills underlying the tasks. Whether the training objectives are defined in terms of tasks or skills depends upon many factors. Foremost among these factors are considerations of whether the tasks reduce meaningfully to skills and whether the training intervention is concentrating upon meeting the immediate needs for task performance or upon long-term benefits derived from equipping personnel with transportable skills (Berenson, Berenson and Carkhuff, 1978; Carkhuff and Berenson, 1981). Increasingly, with the growing emphasis upon human resource development as the source of productivity growth, training programs are emphasizing person-specific skills development. In this work, we are going to define our training objectives. However, depending upon the considerations indicated above, we will sometimes use tasks as well as skills in our examples.

Principles of Training Skill Objectives

The training objective in this lesson is for the *instructional trainees to be able to specify the dimensions of training skill objectives in their areas of expertise. They will learn to do so by asking themselves basic questions, under the formal and informal conditions of training and with varying timelines. The trainers will specify the dimensions of skill objectives at a level that contains all of the ingredients necessary to insure performance of the skills.*

Before you learn to define training skill objectives, you may want an index of your present skill level in this area. Take some objectives of your area of training expertise and outline how you would define the objectives in observable and measurable terms.

_____

_____

_____

_____

_____

Indexing Training Skill Objectives

You did well if you described the activities or behaviors that your trainees will perform. We use the following terms: components, functions, processes, conditions and standards. They describe the following operations: *who will do what, by what means, under what conditions and to what standards.*

Components: Who and what things are involved?
Functions: What will be done?
Processes: How will they be done?
Conditions: Where, when and why will they be done?
Standards: How well will they be done?

The components, functions, processes, conditions and standards define the operations of the training skill objectives around which the training will be designed.

Overviewing Training Skill Objectives

Components

The components of a training skill objective describe its basic ingredients. Components are always nouns describing persons, data or things involved in the desired performance. The most important component in any training skill objective is the person who needs to acquire and use the skill. Sometimes other ingredients, like special tools or materials, machinery or computers are involved. However, these are usually elaborated upon by the other dimensions of training skill objectives. Our training skill objective is always a statement of what our trainees will be able to do when they complete the skill steps. Therefore, trainee performance is the end result of training.

Defining Components

The primary components in any training skill objective must be the recipients of the training experience. In training employees, the recipient population is always the employee-trainees. Similarly, in education, the recipient population is always the learners or students. You, as a trainer being trained in content preparation, are our trainee and therefore, our recipient. For example, we may state the trainees' role as recipients in terms of their relationship with other ingredients as follows:

> *Given the supervisory data, the supervisory trainees...*
> *Given the computer equipment, the programmer trainees...*
> *Given the productivity goals and the data from the front-end analysis, the ISD (Instructional Systems Design) trainees...*

Examples of Basic Ingredients

It might be helpful for you to identify the main components of a training skill objective in your training specialty. Be sure to begin with the trainees as the primary ingredients. Add any other people, data or things components that are essential to achieving the training skill objective. While this task may appear simple, remember the first step in any training program should be so simple as to seem absurd.

COMPONENTS:

_____

_____

_____

_____

_____

Listing Components

Functions

The functions of a training skill objective describe the desired behaviors the trainees will perform. The functions are always verbs which describe the desired behavioral outcomes of training. Typically, in both the private and public sectors, employee behaviors may be seen at three different levels: duties or responsibilities; tasks to be performed to discharge the duties; skills comprising the tasks. Usually, instructional design personnel address the task level. Increasingly, they are coming to address the skill level because of its long-term benefits. With constantly changing job requirements, skilled personnel are more likely to transfer their skills from one job context to another. In this text, we will define training skill objectives at both skill and task levels, depending upon the simplicity of the tasks, i.e., whether they can be broken down meaningfully into underlying skills.

Defining Functions

For example, we may derive training skill objectives in training for supervisory duties as follows:

Task: Planning Work

Skill Objective Areas:
1. Developing work content
2. Developing delivery plans
3. Relating interpersonally
4. Developing directions

The components and functions of each of these supervisory work planning skill areas may be defined as follows:

1. **Components:** The supervisory trainees
   Functions: will develop work content.

2. **Components:** The supervisory trainees
   Functions: will develop delivery plans.

3. **Components:** The supervisory trainees
   Functions: will relate interpersonally to their supervisees.

4. **Components:** The supervisory trainees
   Functions: will deliver supervisory directions.

Examples of Trainee Activities

As with components, you might find it helpful to practice describing the functions of your specialty training skill objective. Remember to define the trainee's involvement as a behavioral outcome using an action verb or behavior.

COMPONENTS:

_____

_____

_____

_____

_____

FUNCTIONS:

_____

_____

_____

_____

_____

Listing Functions

Processes

The processes in training skill objective describe the means for performing the skill. The processes are adverbial phrases that modify the functions of the training skill objectives. Usually, the description of the means is a straightforward account of the activities necessary to achieve the desired behavioral outcome. In this regard, the processes will become the sources of the skills needed to achieve the training objective. Sometimes special methods or alternative procedures are described that will achieve the desired outcome. Special methods and alternative procedures are usually specified if there are contingencies that can affect the outcome. Most of these are contextual or environmental. When such is the case, the context and the means specific to that context are described.

Defining Processes

The processes of the training skill objective define how the trainees will achieve the functions. For example, the processes of training skill objectives for supervisory work planning functions may be defined as follows:

1. **Components:** The supervisory trainees
   Functions: will develop work content
   Processes: by identifying work objectives and the major tasks required to reach those objectives.

2. **Components:** The supervisory trainees
   Functions: will develop delivery plans
   Processes: by analyzing responsibility for activities and tasks, designating timelines and identifying the expected level of effort.

3. **Components:** The supervisory trainees
   Functions: will relate interpersonally to their supervisees
   Processes: by responding to their experience and giving direction to their tasks.

4. **Components:** The supervisory trainees
   Functions: will deliver supervisory directions
   Processes: by directing what is to be done, by whom, as well as how, when, where and how well it is to be done.

Examples of Processes

You may wish to practice describing the processes of your specialty training skill objective. Remember to emphasize the means by which the processes will be performed. Build your definition cumulatively.

COMPONENTS:

_____

_____

_____

_____

FUNCTIONS:

_____

_____

_____

_____

PROCESSES:

_____

_____

_____

_____

Listing Processes

Conditions

The conditions in a training skill objective describe the contingencies under which the functions will be performed. The conditions are also adverbial phrases. They tell us where and when the functions are to be performed. The conditions describe the context in which the performance takes place. The context of the training skill objective becomes increasingly important as trainees start to transfer their skills from one environment to another. For example, the training context is the training room. However, the training context is varied to better approximate the actual work environment in which the trainees will work. The "when" aspect of conditions states the beginning and end of the training skill objective timeline. Timelines tell us when to observe or measure the behavior and determine if the training skill objective was achieved within the desired time.

Defining Conditions

The conditions of the training skill objective, then, describe where and when the trainees perform the skill. For example, with the emphasis upon improving individual performance through supervision, the conditions may shift from routine on-the-job, "after-crisis" supervision conditions to proactive crisis prevention conditions.

1. **Components:** The supervisory trainees
   Functions: will develop work content
   Processes: by identifying work objectives and the major tasks required to reach those objectives
   Conditions: before and during job performance to prevent crises.

2. **Components:** The supervisory trainees
   Functions: will develop delivery plans
   Processes: by analyzing responsibility for activities and tasks, designating timelines and identifying the expected level of effort
   Conditions: before and during job performance to prevent crises.

Examples of Contextual Conditions

3. **Components:** The supervisory trainees
   Functions: will relate interpersonally to their supervisees
   Processes: by responding to their experience and giving direction to their tasks
   Conditions: before and during job performance to prevent crises.

4. **Components:** The supervisory trainees
   Functions: will deliver supervisory directions
   Processes: by directing what is to be done, by whom, as well as how, when, where and how well it is to be done
   Conditions: before and during job performance to prevent crises.

Examples of Contextual Conditions

You may wish to practice describing the conditions of your specialty training skill objective. Remember to describe where and when the trainees will perform the training skill objective. Continue to build your definition cumulatively.

COMPONENTS:

_____

_____

_____

FUNCTIONS:

_____

_____

_____

PROCESSES:

_____

_____

_____

CONDITIONS:

_____

_____

_____

Listing Conditions

Standards

The standards in a training skill objective describe the desired level of excellence to be achieved. Standards are adverbial phrases which allow us to judge the effectiveness of our performance of the skill. In the case of putting a person on the moon, the absolute standards of getting to the moon and back in good health defined the efficacy of the Apollo Space Program. In training environments, standards may be absolute as indicated by the presence of certain behaviors or responses. Usually, however, during the acquisition stage of training, standards are often relative, describing the number or percentage of correct actions or responses.

Defining Standards

The standards of the training skill objective, then, describe how well the trainees perform the skill. For example, the supervisory work planning standards may be stated as follows:

1. **Components:** The supervisory trainees
   Functions: will develop work content
   Processes: by identifying work objectives and the major tasks required to reach those objectives
   Conditions: before and during job performance to prevent crises
   Standards: at a level where employees can identify and carry out the related subtasks.

2. **Components:** The supervisory trainees
   Functions: will develop delivery plans
   Processes: by analyzing responsibility for activities and tasks, designating timelines and identifying the expected
   Conditions: level of effort
   before and during job performance
   Standards: to prevent crises
   at a level where a realistic manner of reaching the work objective is described.

Examples of Levels of Excellence

3. **Components:** The supervisory trainees
   Functions: will relate interpersonally to their supervisees
   Processes: by responding to their experience and giving direction to their tasks
   Conditions: before and during job performance to prevent crises
   Standards: at levels that relate the employees' experience interchangeably to the tasks-at-hand.

4. **Components:** The supervisory trainees
   Functions: will deliver supervisory directions
   Processes: by directing what is to be done, by whom, as well as how, when, where and how well it is to be done
   Conditions: before and during job performance to prevent crises
   Standards: at levels that enable the employees to implement the directions.

Examples of Levels of Excellence

You may wish to practice describing the standards of your specialty training skill objective. Remember to describe how well the trainees perform the skill. Complete your cumulative definition of your training skill objective.

COMPONENTS:

_____

_____

_____

_____

FUNCTIONS:

_____

_____

_____

_____

Listing Standards

PROCESSES:

_____

_____

_____

_____

CONDITIONS:

_____

_____

_____

_____

STANDARDS:

_____

_____

_____

_____

Listing Standards

Exercises

Thus far, the training skill objective has been defined in terms of the instructional trainees acquiring the skills. In reality, we are preparing the trainees to apply those skills to their actual design tasks. The closer we can approximate the dimensions of the actual job environments in our training, the higher the probability of the trainees successfully applying the skills they have acquired. We can approximate applying the training objective development skills in a number of training situations on the following pages. See if you can develop an example from the realms of human, informational and technical resource development.

Exercising Training Skill Objectives

First, let us try another illustration of a training skill objective in the area of supervision:

Components: Supervisory trainees

Functions: will diagnose task performance

Processes: by diagnosing employee skills and implementation

Conditions: before and during job performance to prevent crises

Standards: at a level where employee skills and skill implementation are accurately described for each individual employee.

Try to develop an example of a training skill objective in your own specialty area or in another area of human resource development.

_____

_____

_____

Repeat Exercise

An example of a training skill objective in the area of information resource development in a computer programmer's work context might be the following:

Components: System analyst trainee

Functions: will design a physical (hardware) system to meet a user's need

Processes: by identifying the tasks to be implemented by the system, analyzing the tasks, and determining requirements for input devices, output devices, central processing unit, mass storage and communication

Conditions: while working within a variety of different time and cost constraints

Standards: at a level where the physical system meets the needs of the specified user as measured by that user's ability to implement the identified tasks under the agreed-upon conditions.

Try to develop an example of a training skill objective in an information resource development area:

_____

_____

_____

Repeat Exercise
_____

Still another example of applying training skill objectives to technical resource development involves quality assurance personnel:

Components: The piece part inspector trainee

Functions: will measure each base plate's critical tolerance areas for accuracy of casting

Processes: by print reading, surface determination and venier caliper calibration, and by conducting a surface caliper check

Conditions: while conducting piece part inspection of cast base plates at the vendor production facility

Standards: within specified timeline and with 100% accuracy of measure.

You may want to try to develop an example of a training skill objective in a technical resource development area:

_____

_____

_____

Repeat Exercise

You may wish to practice applying the use of training skill objectives in your training specialty. How many different kinds of job-related applications can you make? Can you make any to a home context or an educational context?

_____

_____

_____

_____

_____

Application Exercise

Summary

Perhaps you can again take some aspect of your training specialty and outline how you would specify the training skill objectives. This will give you an index of how well you learned your content:

_____

_____

_____

If you are able to break down your training skill objectives into their productive dimensions, then we have accomplished our training skill objective:

Components: The instructional trainees

Functions: will specify the dimensions of skill objectives

Processes: by asking basic questions

Conditions: under formal and informal conditions

Standards: at a 99% level of accuracy

Indexing Training Skill Objectives

If you have accomplished our training skill objective, then you should be quite pleased with yourself. You are now capable of productively planning your training skill objectives in your specialty area:

Components: Who is involved?

Functions: What will they do?

Processes: How will they do them?

Conditions: Where and when will they do them?

Standards: How well will they do them?

You will also be capable of "thinking on your feet" as you receive new or changing information input. Indeed, you can teach the skill definition process to your trainees. Ultimately, the trainees will need to learn how to define training skill objectives in appropriate areas of their work.

LEVELS OF CONTENT
  Skills:
  Components
  Functions
  Processes
  Conditions
  Standards

Summarizing Training Skill Objectives

Defining a training skill objective is the most profound act of training. Indeed, defining an objective is the most profound act for any activity of humankind. From the largest perspective, developing a skill objective is a major step toward achieving any goal in our lives. The skill objective makes it possible for the entrepreneur to transform a dream into achievable terms. The skill objective makes it possible to train for success and competence in any area. It makes "throwing out a skyhook" literally possible. Just ask the Apollo astronauts! Any goal that can be conceived can be operationally defined. Any goal that can be operationalized can be achieved.

References

Berenson, D.H., Berenson, S.R. and Carkhuff, R.R. *The Skills of Teaching—Content Development Skills.* Amherst, Mass.: Human Resource Development Press, 1978.

Carkhuff, R.R. and Berenson, D.H. *The Skilled Teacher.* Amherst, Mass.: Human Resource Development Press, 1981.

French, R.F. *Preparing Instructional Objectives.* San Francisco, Calif.: Fearon Publishers, 1957.

Kearny, N.C. *Elementary School Objectives.* New York: Russell Sage Foundation, 1953.

Mager, R.F. *Preparing Instructional Objectives.* San Francisco, Calif.: Fearon Publishers, 1962.

Mager, R.F. *Developing Attitude Toward Learning.* San Francisco, Calif.: Fearon Publishers, 1968.

Mager, R.F. *Goal Analysis.* San Francisco, Calif.: Fearon Publishers, 1972.

Odiorne, G. *Training by Objectives.* Marshfield, Mass.: Pitman Press, 1965.

Pipe, P. *Objectives—Tools for Change.* San Francisco, Calif.: Fearon Publishers, 1975.

5

Developing Skill Steps

Not everything about achieving the training skill is an exciting adventure. Once the training skill objective is defined, skill steps must be developed to achieve that objective. The skill steps are derived from the training skill objective. Skill steps constitute the often complex follow-through program that is the basis for achieving our training skill objective. Developing skill steps is when we get down to the "nitty gritty" things that make us successful in achieving our objectives. For example, having defined the objective of putting a person on the moon, NASA became involved in the long, arduous process of developing the mechanical steps needed in order to accomplish the lunar landing operations. The otherwise painful journey was made joyful by the sense of accomplishment that accompanied the achievement of each sub-objective.

Review and Overview

Often the skill steps are dictated by the processes helping to define the training skill objective. When the processes are precise about the methods to be employed to perform the function, the skill steps are determined. When the processes are not precise, content expertise must be developed in order to identify the skill steps.

In general, trainees are most effective in developing the content and skills to be presented when the content and skills are broken down into the smallest possible steps for presentation to the trainees (Brainard, 1976; Butler, 1972; Gagne, 1977; Lumsdaine, 1964; Odiorne, 1965; Smith and Moore, 1962). The smaller the steps the higher the probability of the trainees successfully accomplishing them. Put another way, to leave out a step is to increase the probability of the trainees' failure. Indeed, the initial step should be so simple as to be experienced as absurd (Berenson, Berenson and Carkhuff, 1978; Bronson, 1975; Carkhuff and Berenson, 1981; Silvern, 1972; Warren, 1979). This breakdown of content and skills into steps is especially essential in the Information Age where workers must constantly be learning new and changing content (Ausebel, 1978; Wheaton and Mirabella, 1972).

Principles of Skill Steps

The training skill objective in this lesson is as follows:

The instructional trainees will develop skill steps by breaking the content down into atomistic steps under formal and informal conditions with steps small enough for all trainees to perform.

Before you learn to develop your skill steps, you might want an index of your skills in this area. Perhaps you can develop the skill step content to achieve your specialty training skill objective. Outline how you would develop the steps in achievable terms.

_____

_____

_____

_____

_____

Indexing Skill Steps

You did well if you emphasized all the steps that your trainee must perform in order to achieve the stated training skill objective. These steps would include the things a trainee must do and think about.

DO Steps: The major actions the trainee must perform

DO Substeps: The substeps of the major actions the trainees must perform

BEFORE THINK Steps: The things the trainees must consider before doing the steps

DURING THINK Steps: The things the trainees must consider while doing the steps

AFTER THINK Steps: The things the trainees must consider after doing the steps

The *do* steps and *think* steps define the development of the skill steps that lead to achieving the training skill objective.

Overviewing Skill Steps

Do Steps

Do steps are developed by listing the major steps the trainee will need to *do* to perform the skill. The first step should tell trainees where to begin. The final step should culminate in the achievement of the training skill objective. The intermediary steps provide all the instructions the trainees need in order to do the skill correctly. One way to develop *do* steps is to begin with the simplest step for the trainees to perform. Then we can sequence the steps by contingency: each step is contingent upon performance of the previous steps. In Book II, we will learn to sequence in other ways to individualize the training delivery. Make sure the first step is so simple that any trainee can perform it.

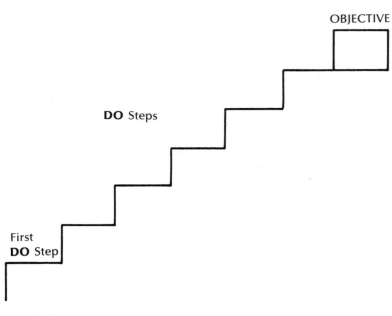

OBJECTIVE

DO Steps

First
DO Step

Developing Do Steps

The basic questions in developing the skill steps is how the trainees will accomplish the training skill objectives: How do the trainees *do* the skill? For example, if we want trainees to replace empty carbon dioxide cannisters, then one of the first things the trainees must do is learn how to discriminate between empty and full cannisters. Similarly, if we want trainees to put stock items into stock bins properly, then one of the first things might be to discriminate one stock item from another. If we are providing training in interpersonal communication skills, as one of our supervisory training objectives, we might answer the "how" question as follows:

> *OBJECTIVE:* Trainees will communicate interpersonally by getting the other's perspective, giving their own perspective, merging differences and going to action, in formal and informal situations, so well that all involved points of view are expressed and considered.
>
> **DO** Steps: 1. Getting another's perspective
>   2. Giving your own perspective
>   3. Merging differences
>   4. Going to action

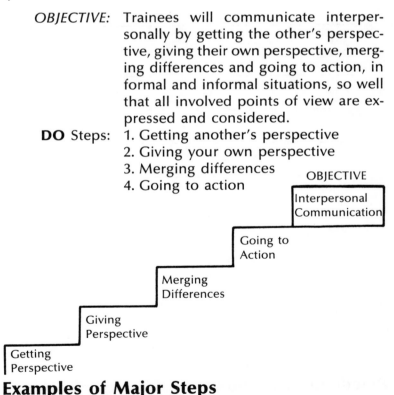

Examples of Major Steps

You may wish to practice developing *do* steps to achieve your specialty training skill objective. Be sure to emphasize how the trainees will *do* the skill.

OBJECTIVE:

_____

_____

_____

_____

_____

DO Steps:

_____

_____

_____

_____

_____

Practicing Do Steps

Do Substeps

In developing skill steps, it is important to recognize that many things that are automatic for us are not automatic for the trainees. We may have performed the skill so many times that we have mastered it. It is critical that we make all the steps involved explicit to ensure the trainees' achievement of the training skill objective. *Do* substeps are one way we bridge the skill gaps and increase trainees' ability to perform the training skill objective. *Do* substeps are mini-steps that make up the performance of each major step. They are developed in precisely the same way as the *do* steps. You just treat each *do* step as if it were a training skill objective. Then develop the first substep followed by intermediary substeps.

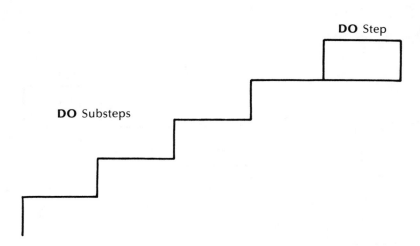

DO Step

DO Substeps

Developing Do Substeps

We continue to ask the "how" question in developing our *do* substeps. For example, in replacing empty carbon dioxide cannisters, the trainees must detach a cannister before determining the amount of its contents. Also, in discriminating stock items, one must have the item present. If we are training in "getting perspective" skills, then there are several *do* substeps that trainees must perform to get the other's perspective.

DO Step: Getting another person's perspective

DO Substeps: 1. Demonstrate attention (attend) to the person.
               2. Observe the person.
               3. Listen to the message.
               4. Verbally reflect the other's message.

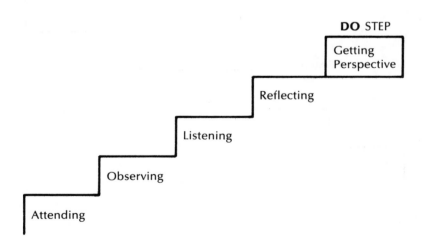

Examples of Minor Steps

Again, you may want to practice developing *do* substeps to achieve your specialty training skill objective. Continue to describe how the trainees will actually *do* the skill.

OBJECTIVE:

_____

_____

_____

DO Step:

_____

_____

_____

DO Substeps:

_____

_____

_____

Practicing Do Substeps

Before Think Steps

Just when we think we have all the skill steps, we find there are still other questions about performing the skill. The answers to these questions can be considered think steps or check steps. They include the items the trainees need to think about *before, during* and *after* each *do* step. Think steps provide ways of checking oneself to ensure the *do* steps are being performed correctly. The *before* think steps determine whether the trainees have all of the resources they need in order to perform the *do* step. For example, if the trainees are replacing empty carbon dioxide cannisters or properly stocking inventory, they need the appropriate materials, gauges, warehouse maps and inventory placement charts.

DO Step

BEFORE THINK Steps

Developing Before Think Steps

To continue our illustration, before performing the *do* step of getting another person's perspective, the trainees may ask the *before* think questions. In general, they ask whether all the necessary resources are available. For example, trainees may ask if the setting in which they will talk with the other person is arranged so as to facilitate communication.

DO Step

Getting Perspective

BEFORE THINK Steps

- Appropriate Setting?
- Appropriate Amount of Time Available?

Examples of Resource Steps

You may wish to practice developing *before* think steps to achieve your specialty training skill objective. Remember to determine that the trainees have all the resources they need to perform the skill steps.

OBJECTIVE:

_____

_____

_____

DO Step:

_____

_____

_____

DO Substeps:

_____

_____

_____

BEFORE THINK Steps:

_____

_____

_____

Practicing Before Think Steps

During Think Steps

During think steps answer the questions concerning whether we are performing the *do* steps correctly. Again, the *during* think steps provide us with an opportunity to check ourselves while we are performing the skill steps. For example, in replacing carbon dioxide cannisters, the trainees may ask whether they have adequately attached the nozzle of the new cartridge. If the trainees are replacing used inventory, they might ask if a particular stock item is low on the inventory sheet.

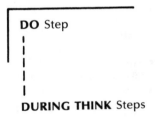

DO Step

DURING THINK Steps

Developing During Think Steps

For example, during the performance of the *do* step of getting perspective, the trainees may ask the *during* think questions: Are they attending? Are they listening to the content? Are they observing feelings? Are they verbally reflecting the content and feelings that they see and hear?

DO STEP

Getting Perspective

DURING THINK Steps

- Attending physically?
- Observing facial expressions and body posture?
- Listening to content and voice tone?
- Reflecting feeling and content?

Example of Check Steps

You may practice developing the *during* think steps for achieving your specialty training skill objective. Be sure to determine how to identify the correctness with which the trainees are performing the skill steps.

OBJECTIVE:

_____

_____

DO Step:

_____

_____

DO Substeps:

_____

_____

BEFORE THINK Steps:

_____

_____

DURING THINK Steps:

_____

_____

Practicing During Think Steps

After Think Steps

After think steps answer the questions concerning the outcome of our performance of the *do* steps. Again, the *after* think steps give us an opportunity to determine how well we performed the skill step. For example, in replacing carbon dioxide cannisters, the trainees may ask whether the antilener arm moved with enough force. If the trainees are replacing inventory, they may ask if they have placed the stock items in the proper stock bins.

AFTER THINK Steps

DO Step

Developing After Think Steps

For example, after the performance of the *do* step of getting perspective, the trainees may ask the *after* think question: Are they able to capture accurately the other person's point of view? If the answer is affirmative, then the trainees are prepared to do the next *do* step of giving their own perspective.

— — — — AFTER THINK Steps

DO Steps

Getting
Perspective

- Accurately captured the other's point of view?

- Reflect in a way the other person could accept?

- Did I sound genuine?

Example of Outcome Steps

You may practice developing your *after* think steps for achieving your specialty training skill objective. Be sure to describe how to determine the correctness of the skill performance.

OBJECTIVE:

_____

_____

DO Step:

_____

_____

DO Substeps:

_____

_____

BEFORE THINK Steps:

_____

_____

DURING THINK Steps:

_____

_____

AFTER THINK Steps:

_____

_____

Practicing After Think Steps

Exercises

Once more we are preparing the instructional trainees to apply their content development skills in their actual work contexts. The closer we can approximate the dimensions of the actual work place in training, the higher the probability of the trainees utilizing the skills they have acquired. For example, we can use interpersonal communication skills for other applications like marketing by approximating those working conditions in the training experience.

Following is an illustration of fully developing the skill steps for a customer service training skill objective.

OBJECTIVE: The Customer Service Representative (CSR) will communicate whenever interacting with customers, by getting the customer's perspective, giving her (or his) own perspective, merging any differences and going on to action at such a level that the customer will feel served.

DO Step 1: Get perspective.
DO Substeps:
1. Attend physically to the customer.
2. Observe the customer.
3. Listen to the customer.
4. Reflect feeling and/or content.

DO Step 2: Give perspective.
DO Substeps:
1. Identify your viewpoint.
2. State viewpoint in specific, genuine and tactful terms.

Exercising Do Steps

DO Step 3:   Merge any differences.
DO Substeps: 1. Identify any differences in points of view.
2. Clarify customer's goal.
3. Clarify values.
4. Identify integrative or compromise solutions.

DO Step 4:   Go on to action.
DO Substeps: 1. Identify what action steps need to be taken.
2. Develop action plan.

Exercising Do Steps

The think steps are as follows:

BEFORE THINK Steps:
- Is the setting appropriate?
- Is the amount of time appropriate?

DURING THINK Steps:
- Is the response to content and feeling accurate?
- Are any differences in perspectives identified?

AFTER THINK Steps:
- Did the action meet the customer's values?
- Was the customer satisfied?

Exercising Think Steps

See if you can develop the skill steps leading to a human resource development training skill objective.

OBJECTIVE: _____

_____

_____

_____

_____

_____

Skill Steps:

Repeat Exercise

An example of developing skill steps for a safety training skill objective follows.

OBJECTIVE: The industrial skills trainees will protect themselves by putting on safety glasses, ear protectors and safety shoes and adequately adjusting clothing while preparing to go out onto the shop floor so that all personal safety attire and adjustments are in place at the beginning of each work shift.

DO Step 1: Put on safety glasses.
DO Substeps: 1. Remove from case.
2. Check for breakage.
3. Check for cleanliness and clear lenses.
4. Place glasses on nose and behind ears.

DO Step 2: Put on ear protectors.
DO Substeps: 1. Remove from container.
2. Roll foam cylinder ear protector between thumb and forefinger until small enough to fit in external ear canal.
3. Insert compressed ear protector into external ear canal.

Exercising Do Steps

DO Step 3: Put on safety shoes.
DO Substeps: 1. Inspect shoes for excess wear or damage.
2. Adequately loosen laces.
3. Insert foot into shoe while holding shoe tongue in one hand and shoe heel in other.
4. Tighten laces.
5. Tie laces with double knot.

DO Step 4: Adjust clothing.
DO Substeps: 1. Remove all jewelry.
2. Roll sleeve above elbow.
3. Insure shirt is adequately buttoned and tucked into pants.
4. Insure belt is adequately fastened and looped.

DO Step 5: Put on proper headgear.
DO Substeps: 1. Put on hair net, if needed.
2. Put on safety hat, if needed.

Exercising Do Steps

The think steps are as follows:

BEFORE THINK Steps:
- Have safety glasses?
- Have ear protectors?
- Have safety shoes?
- Have hair garment?
- Have safety hat?

DURING THINK Steps:
- Safety glasses whole?
- Safety glasses clean?
- Safety shoes in good condition?
- Safety shoes have whole laces?
- Clothing in good condition?
- Safety hat in good condition?

AFTER THINK Steps:
- Glasses on properly?
- Ear protection firmly in place?
- Safety shoes properly tied?
- Shirt sleeves rolled properly?
- Shirt adequately buttoned and tucked in?
- Belt adequately fastened and looped?
- Head gear in place?

Practicing Think Steps

See if you can develop the skill steps leading to another training skill objective.

OBJECTIVE: _____

_____

_____

_____

_____

_____

Skill Steps:

Repeat Exercise

An example of developing skill steps for an emergency service training skill objective follows.

OBJECTIVE: The Emergency Medical Technicians trainees will successfully perform emergency tracheostomies by making an open incision in the cricothyroid membrane when a patient has an airway obstruction that interferes with breathing, in less than two minutes as measured by the patient's adequate ability to breath.

DO Step 1: Locate the cricothyroid membrane.

DO Substeps:
1. Slightly hyperextend the neck.
2. Using fingers, find the two most prominent cartilages at the front of the neck.
3. Locate the soft space between the two prominent cartilages.

DO Step 2: Using a sharp-edged instrument, make a one-inch transverse incision in the skin of the soft space between the cartilages.

DO Substeps:
1. Pull the skin tight on both sides of the trachea.
2. Holding the skin firmly, take the sharp-edged instrument and place it at the spot where the incision is to be made.
3. Make a one-inch incision just through the skin by drawing the instrument across the desired incision location. Repeat if necessary at the same spot until the incision is one-inch long and *through the skin.*

Exercising Do Steps

DO Step 3: Stabilize the larynx.
DO Substeps: 1. Place thumb on one side of incision and middle finger on the other.
  2. Press down firmly until trachea is held in place.
  3. Insert index finger into incision and press firmly against the cricothyroid membrane.

DO Step 4: Cut through the cricothyroid membrane.
DO Substeps: 1. Use index fingernail as guide and place instrument blade point against cricothyroid membrane at a transverse angle.
  2. Work instrument blade through the membrane and into the trachea, avoiding excess pressure and damage to the posterior wall of the trachea.

DO Step 5: Spread the incision in the cricothyroid membrane.
DO Substeps: 1. Turn instrument blade at ninety-degree angle.
  2. If available, substitute a flat, thin or open-ended tubular object to replace instrument, making sure the object is large enough so that it cannot be aspirated.

Exercising Do Steps

The think steps are as follows:

BEFORE THINK Steps:
- Make sure one has sharp-edged and preferably sharp-pointed instrument.
- If available, have a flat, thin or open-ended tubular object available to replace instrument in opening.

DURING THINK Steps:
- Insure finding accurate location between two most prominent cartilages in front of neck.
- Insure cut through skin.
- Insure cut through cricothyroid membrane.
- Insure incision is adequately spread.

AFTER THINK Steps:
- Assure patient is able to breath through incision.
- If person is unable to breath, have all other attempts to help patient breath been tried?

Exercising Think Steps

See if you can develop the skill steps leading to still another training skill objective.

OBJECTIVE: _____

_____

_____

_____

_____

_____

Skill Steps:

Repeat Exercise

You may wish to practice applying the skill steps to your training specialty area. Try to make a variety of job-related applications. Also, try to make some applications to a home context or an educational context.

_____

_____

_____

_____

_____

Application Exercise

Summary

Perhaps you can again take some aspect of your training specialty and outline how you would develop your skill steps to achieve your training skill objective. This will give you an index of how well you learned your content.

_____

_____

_____

_____

_____

If you are able to develop your skill steps effectively, then we have accomplished our training skill objective: *The instructional trainees will develop skill steps by breaking the content down into atomistic steps under formal and informal conditions with steps small enough for all trainees to perform.*

Indexing Skill Steps

If you have achieved our training skill objective, then you will be confident in productively developing your skill steps to achieve your skill objectives in your training specialty.

DO Steps: Major Actions
DO Substeps: Mini-Actions
BEFORE THINK Steps: Resources
DURING THINK Steps: Correctness
AFTER THINK Steps: Performance

You will also be capable of "thinking on your feet" to fill the missing skill steps in any training content. You might also want to teach your trainees the skill development process in order to prepare them to develop programs to achieve their personal skill objectives in their work.

LEVELS OF CONTENT
    Skills
    Skill Steps
    DO Steps
    DO Substeps
    BEFORE THINK Steps
    DURING THINK Steps
    AFTER THINK Steps

Summarizing Skill Steps

Skill steps, then, are the mechanical actions we do on the way to our training skill objectives. They are often sheer drudgery to develop and implement. Yet our skill steps are the price we pay to achieve our goals. They are the demands which we make of ourselves that test our commitments to achieving our goals. Just as these training modules are the price of our commitment to trainers so are your training modules the price of your commitment to your trainees. In the words of one master trainer, "The skill steps are a journey through hell on our way to our heavenly objectives." We can put people into the outer reaches of our heavenly experience and we can put trainees into the inner spaces of job mastery. It all depends upon the detail in our skill step training programs.

References

Ausebel, D.P. *Educational Psychology.* New York: Holt, Rinehart and Winston, 1978.

Berenson, D.H., Berenson, S.R. and Carkhuff, R.R. *The Skills of Teaching—Content Development Skills.* Amherst, Mass.: Human Resource Development Press, 1978.

Brainard, C.J. "Learning Research in Piagetian Theory." Chapter in L.S. Siegel and C.J. Brainard (Eds.), *Alternatives to Piaget: Critical Essays on the Theory.* Hillsdale, N.J.: Eribaum, 1976.

Bronson, R.K. *Inservice Procedures for Instructional Systems Development.* Tallahassee, Fla.: Center for Educational Technology, 1975.

Butler, F.C. *Instructional System Development for Vocational and Technical Training.* Englewood Cliffs, N.J.: Educational Technology Publications, 1972.

Carkhuff, R.R. and Berenson, D.H. *The Skilled Teacher.* Amherst, Mass.: Human Resource Development Press, 1981.

Gagne, R.M. *Conditions of Learning.* New York: Holt, Rinehart and Winston, 1977.

Lumsdaine, A.A. Educational Technology, Programmed Learning and Instructional Science. In *Theories of Learning and Instruction.* Chicago, Ill.: National Society for the Study of Education, 1964.

Odiorne, G. *Training by Objectives.* Marshfield, Mass: Pittman Press, 1965.

Silvern, L. *Systems Engineering Applied for Training.* Houston, Tex.: Gulf Publishing, 1972.

Smith, W.I. and Moore, J.W. "Size of Step and Caring." *Psychological Reports,* 1962, 10, 287–294.

Warren, M. *Training for Results.* Reading, Mass.: Addison-Wesley, 1979.

Wheaton, G.R. and Mirabella, A. *Effects of Task Index Variations on Training Effectiveness Criteria.* Silver Spring, Md.: American Institute for Research, 1972.

6

Developing Supportive Knowledge

Knowledge is a necessary but insufficient condition for skill acquisition. Because we know about something does not necessarily mean we can do it. At the same time, knowledge about an operation can help a person learn how to do an operation. Knowing what things are involved, knowing what the purpose is and understanding the principles of the process to be used can facilitate a person's performance of the skill steps. When NASA developed the spacecraft parts to accomplish the lunar landing operations, they required a detailed labeling process that identified a part by its function. Without the ability to identify what the parts were and what they did, such amazing human accomplishments could not have occurred.

Review and Overview

Skills and knowledge do not necessarily follow from each other (Bloom, 1982; Cenci, 1966; Mager, 1962; Odiorne, 1965). Ryle (1949) referred to the distinction between stating factual propositions, "knowing that," and performing skills, "knowing how." Facts, concepts and principles do not necessarily produce skills unless trainers actually learn how to translate them into skills (Brush and Licata, 1983; Carkhuff, 1983; Kaya, Gerhard, Staslewski and Berenson, 1967; Mallory, 1982). Similarly, skills-building does not always incorporate necessary supportive knowledge unless trainers learn how to do so (Berenson, Berenson and Carkhuff, 1978; Bloom, 1982; Gagne, 1977; Gilbert, 1978). In general, knowledge is helpful to trainees when it facilitates skill performance. Knowledge is most helpful when facts and concepts are integrated into principles that lead to training skill objectives (Carkhuff and Berenson, 1981; Gagne, 1977; Moscowitz, 1982). The ability to produce these principles and infer from them the training skill objectives is most critical in the Age of Information (American Management Association, 1980; Martin, 1982).

Principles of Supportive Knowledge

The training skill objective for this lesson is as follows:

The instructional trainees will develop supportive knowledge for skill step performance by breaking the knowledge down into factual and conceptual levels under formal and informal conditions so that knowledge culminates into principles that can be transformed into training skill objectives.

Before you learn to develop your supportive knowledge, you may want an index of your skills in this area. Perhaps you can develop the supportive knowledge to support your skill performance in your training specialty area. Outline how you would develop the knowledge in achievable terms.

_____

_____

_____

_____

_____

Indexing Supportive Knowledge

You did well if you emphasized the supportive knowledge trainees must know to perform a training skill objective. This knowledge needs to include the facts, concepts and principles involved.

Facts: The components, functions and processes to be used in the skill operation.

Concepts: The relationships among the components, functions and processes to be used in the skill operation.

Principles: The implications of the facts and concepts as they relate to the training skill objective.

You may already see the special relationship between these definitions of knowledge and the definitions used to define the training skill objective. Components, functions and processes define the training skill objective in the most broad terms. Facts, concepts and principles define the knowledge that substantiates the performance of the skill steps leading to the training skill objective.

Overviewing Supportive Knowledge

Facts

Facts are the labels attached to persons, places, things or ideas, their purposes and their activities. We use facts as a way of identifying any of these items so that they are commonly understood. If we think of facts as components, functions and processes, they can live for us. They become people loving one another by doing things for each other. They become people and machines making products or other machines through an elaborate set of operations. If we did not know the names of the people, the machines, what they made or how they worked, we could not describe the magic of working or even the workings of magic.

> *OBJECTIVE:* The operations to be performed at the desired level in the specified context.
>
> Skill Steps: The steps the trainees need to do.
>
> **Facts:** The names of the components, functions and processes involved in the skill steps.

Developing Facts

Facts are significant in relation to skills. They name the components, functions and processes of the skills or skill steps. The very process in which we are engaged is one of identifying facts. Labeling things as facts, concepts, principles and skill objectives is a process of identifying facts. The facts we train our trainees are those related to the performance of the skills we teach them. We relate our facts to skill performance by asking ourselves: "Does the trainee need to know this fact to do this skill?" and "Will knowing this fact help the trainee to do this skill better?" Teaching the supportive facts will help us to keep our content relevant.

Skill Step 1. _____

Facts: _____

Skill Step 2. _____

Facts: _____

Skill Step 3. _____

Facts: _____

Identifying Facts

For example, we may identify certain facts in training new sales personnel in interpersonal communication with customers. In training interpersonal communication skills our trainees must know what the components, functions and processes of the communication skills are before they can relate effectively to customers. (Keep in mind that only those facts that might be difficult for the trainee to understand need to be presented—not every fact.)

> *OBJECTIVE:* Customer Service Representatives (CSRs) will communicate interpersonally by getting the customer's perspective, communicating their own perspective, merging differences and going to action, in all customer contacts, at a level that insures the customer is heard and feels served.

> Skill Step 1. Get customer's perspective.
> **Facts:** Attending physically, observing, listening, reflecting.

> Skill Step 2. Give your own perspective.
> **Facts:** Specificity, genuineness, respect.

> Skill Step 3. Merge any differences in perspectives.
> **Facts:** Goals, values, integrative solutions, compromise solutions, accommodation.

> Skill Step 4. Go on to action.
> **Facts:** Action plan.

Example of Identifying Facts

We can develop facts in any specialty training area and at any level of content detail. For example, in the training of employees in the operation of an inventory system, one step is the restocking of inventory items. We can identify the related substeps and factual supportive knowledge.

Skill Step:	Place replacement inventory items in stock bins.
Skill Substep 1.	Identify number of inventory items needed to fill inventory bin.
Facts:	Full bin.
Skill Substep 2.	Move inventory items presently in stock bin to front of bin.
Facts:	Current inventory items.
Skill Substep 3.	Place new inventory items to the rear of the inventory items in the stock bin.
Facts:	New inventory items.

Developing Facts in a Specialty Area

Perhaps you may wish to practice developing the facts to support your trainees' performance of skill steps. Be sure to emphasize the labels of the components, functions and processes of the skills or skill steps.

Skill Steps: _____

Facts: _____

_____

Skill Substep 1. _____

Facts: _____

_____

Skill Substep 2. _____

Facts: _____

_____

Skill Substep 3. _____

Facts: _____

_____

Practicing Supportive Facts

Concepts

Perhaps the most exciting level of content involves the development of concepts. There are no boundaries to our concepts of our personal future or of humanity's ingenuity. It is like the new employee's fantasy of promotion and career success, or the fantasies presented for a company's future in its annual report. There is another level of concept development that begins to integrate the supportive knowledge we have developed. For example, when NASA started to identify how the spacecraft parts related to the desired functions of certain objectives, it was building the concepts of the lunar landing operation. In other words, it not only described the components, functions and processes but also described their relationship to one another within a particular step in the operation. Each concept provided, on a small scale, the same excitement that was accomplished by the final mission.

Skill Steps:	The steps the trainees need to do.
Facts:	The components, functions and processes to be used in the skill operation.
Concepts:	The relationships among the components, functions and processes to be used in the skill operation.

Developing Concepts

Concepts describe how various facts affect one another. They answer the question "How do these facts relate to one another?" Conceptual learning enables trainees to organize what they know. Concepts are easy to identify—they are what most of us communicate in our conversations. Usually we build concepts by association or by relating facts in terms of how they affect each other. For example, "Tom supervises John" says that one person (a component) supervises another person (a component) in job task performance (a function).

Skill Step 1. _____

Concepts: _____

Skill Step 2. _____

Concepts: _____

Skill Step 3. _____

Concepts: _____

Identifying Concepts

In practice, concepts tell us how facts fit together. Concepts should describe how a set of identified components, functions and processes are combined. Like facts, concepts take on significance in relation to skills. We relate concepts to skill performance by asking "Do the trainees need to know the concepts to do the skill?"

One way of presenting concepts of skill steps is in "cause-and-effect" relationships: "If ___(cause)___ , then ___(effect)___ ." Another way of presenting concepts is in correlational relationships: "If ___(cause)___ , then ___(effect)___ tends to follow." For example, in teaching effective writing we might present the following concepts:

> "If you outline your manual before writing it, then your chapters will be sequenced contingently in writing."

> "If you outline your chapters before writing them, then your steps will build upon each other in each chapter."

> "If you write a topic sentence for your paragraph, then you will identify the main idea of the paragraph."

Defining Concepts

For example, in training new sales personnel in communicating interpersonally with customers, the trainees must understand certain concepts regarding the dynamics of interpersonal relations and nonverbal communication before they can do the steps.

OBJECTIVE: Customer Service Representatives (CSRs) will communicate interpersonally by getting the customer's perspective, communicating their own perspective, merging differences and going to action, in all customer contacts, at a level that insures the customer is heard and feels served.

Skill Step 1. Get customer's perspective.
Concepts: If the CSR gets the customer's perspective, then she (or he) will understand the customer.

Skill Step 2. Give your own perspective.
Concepts: If the CSR gives the customer her (or his) perspective, then the customer will have additional information.

Skill Step 3. Merge any differences in perspectives.
Concepts: If the CSR works to merge any differences in perspectives, then action will be taken that meets the customer's needs.

Skill Step 4. Go on to action.
Concepts: If the CSR develops a specific plan of action for the customer, then the planned action can be monitored.

Example of Concepts

We can develop supportive concepts in any specialty training area and at any level of content detail. For example, in inventory control, when replacing inventory items, we may develop the following supportive concepts at the sub-step level:

Do Step: Place replacement inventory items in stock bins.

Do Substep 1. Identify number of inventory items needed to fill stock bin.

Concepts: If the employee subtracts the number of inventory items presently in the bin from the total number the bin holds, then the employee will be able to discriminate the number of inventory items needed.

Do Substep 2. Move inventory items presently in stock bin to front of bin.

Concepts: If the employee moves the inventory items presently in the stock bin to the front of the bin, then the person will have adequate room for the new inventory items at the rear, while assuring the oldest inventory items will be used first.

Do Substep 3. Place new inventory items to the rear of the inventory items in the stock bin.

Concepts: If the employee places the specified number of new inventory items to the rear of the inventory items in the stock bin, then he or she will fill the stock bin to capacity.

Developing Concepts in a Specialty Area

You may choose to practice developing the concepts to support the trainees' performance of skill steps or skill substeps. Be sure to emphasize the relationships among the components, functions and processes.

Skill Steps: _____

Concepts: _____

_____

Skill Substep 1. _____

Concepts: _____

_____

Skill Substep 2. _____

Concepts: _____

_____

Skill Substep 3. _____

Concepts: _____

_____

Practicing Supportive Concepts

Principles

The level of cognitive development that is most uniquely human is the level of principles. Principles organize our facts and concepts around their purposes. They enable us to interpret our worlds and validate the relationships we create among the facts. This validation occurs when our specified facts and concepts achieve the stated purpose. In this manner, principles not only account for past relationships, but also allow us to infer new relationships. For example, Frederick Taylor's principle that understanding time and motion of a job task allows us to improve an employee's productivity is applied again and again by industrial engineers in designing new machinery.

The entire lunar landing operation was based upon principles of the physical sciences. One set of phenomena was functionally related to another. All phenomena were related to the total space mission of putting a person on the moon. Without the functional relationships described by scientific principles, the Apollo Program could not have taken place. Principles are our theoretical models for how and why something is taking place. They help us to understand, in some way, our universe. We ultimately test that understanding in our human experiences.

Skill Steps: The steps the trainees need to do.
Facts: The components, functions and processes to be used in the skill operation.
Concepts: The relationships among the components, functions and processes to be used in the skill operation.
Principles: The implications of the facts and concepts as they relate to the training skill

Developing Principles

There are many principles related to every skill we teach. The most important principles describe how and why something works. Most principles deal with the implications of the cause-and-effect or correlational relationships of the concepts: "If __(cause)__ , then __(effect)__ so that __(implication)__ ." For example, in teaching effective writing we might present the following principles.

"If you outline your paper before writing it, then your ideas will build upon each other so that the paper will have a logical flow and coherent organization."

"If you write a topic sentence for your paragraph, then you will identify the main idea of the paragraph so that the other sentences of the paragraph will relate to the paragraph topic."

A simple way of understanding a supportive principle is in terms of trainee benefits of achieving a training skill objective:

"If __(skill steps)__ , then __(training skill objective)__ so that __(trainee benefits)__ ."

For example, in training meter readers:

"If you read the kilowatt hour cyclometer pointer electric meter from left to right reading the first cyclometer as it turns clockwise, the second counterclockwise, the third clockwise, then you

Defining Principles

will get a reading of the amount of electricity consumed so that you can compare it to a previous reading to determine the incidence of consumption."

Skill Step 1. _____

Principles: _____

Skill Step 2. _____

Principles: _____

Skill Step 3. _____

Principles: _____

Defining Principles

Like facts and concepts, principles take on significance in relation to skills. We relate principles to skill performance by asking: "Do the trainees need to know the principle to do the skill?"

For example, in training new sales personnel in attending physically, the trainees must understand certain principles incorporating the facts and concepts relative to the achievement of the training skill objective.

> *OBJECTIVE:* Customer Service Representatives (CSRs) will communicate interpersonally by getting the customer's perspective, communicating their own perspective, merging differences and going to action, in all customer contacts, at a level that insures the customer is heard and feels served.

> Skill Step 1. Get customer's perspective.
> **Principles:** If the CSR gets the customer's perspective, then she (or he) will understand the customer so that the CSR has information needed to serve or persuade the customer.

> Skill Step 2. Give your own perspective.
> **Principles:** If the CSR gives the customer her (or his) perspective, then the customer will have additional information so that the customer is better served.

Example of Supportive Principles

Skill Step 3.   Merge any differences in perspectives.
Principles: If the CSR works to merge any differences in perspectives, then action will be taken that meets the customer's needs so that the opportunity for repeat business is enhanced.

Skill Step 4.   Go on to action.
Principles: If the CSR develops a specific action plan for the customer, then the planned action can be monitored so that the CSR insures the customer is served.

Example of Supportive Principles

We can develop the supportive principles in any specialty training area and at any level of content development. For example, in inventory control, when replacing inventory items we may develop the following supportive principles at the substep level:

Skill Step: Place replacement inventory items in stock bins.

Skill Substep 1. Identify number of inventory items needed to fill stock bin.
Principles: If the employee subtracts the number of inventory items presently in the bin from the total number the bin holds, then the employee will be able to discriminate the number of inventory items needed so that the number can be requested and the number of trips to the main warehouse can be reduced.

Skill Substep 2. Move inventory items presently in stock bin to front of bin.
Principles: If the employee moves the inventory items presently in the stock bin to the front of the bin, then the person will have adequate room for the new inventory items at the rear, while assuring the oldest inventory items will be used first so that spoilage of the inventory items due to age will not occur.

Developing Principles in a Specialty Area

Skill Substep 3. Place new inventory items to the rear of the inventory items in the stock bin.

Principles: If the employee places the specified number of new inventory items to the rear in the stock bin, then the employee will fill the stock bin to capacity so that the production line will not run out.

Developing Principles in a Specialty Area

You may choose to practice developing principles to support your trainees' performance of skill steps or skill substeps. Use the format: "If ___, then ___ so that ___."

Skill Step: _____

Principles: _____

_____

_____

Skill Substep 1. _____

Principles: _____

_____

_____

Skill Substep 2. _____

Principles: _____

_____

_____

Skill Substep 3. _____

Principles: _____

_____

Practicing Supportive Principles

Exercises

We are training individuals to apply the skills they learn in their actual work settings. The knowledge serves to support the application of the skill steps. Factual and conceptual knowledge support skill step performance. Principles help to explain the purpose of the skill step and supportive knowledge as it relates to the trainee skill objective and/or overall productivity goal. An example of developing supportive knowledge for human resource development might involve the following trainee skill objective.

> *OBJECTIVE:* Technical trainers will personalize trainees' learning experiences by relating the training content to individual trainee problems and learning goals throughout the training process. Each trainee will understand how learning the training objective will be useful to him/her in the performance of his/her job.

> Skill Steps: 1. Identify individual trainee problems.
> 2. Identify individual trainee goals.
> 3. Relate training content to the individual problems and goals.

Exercising Supportive Knowledge

Principles:	If the technical trainer personalizes trainees' learning experience, then trainees will know specifically what they need to learn or improve so that they will be able to better accomplish their job task.
Concepts:	If the trainer can assist the trainee in identifying the trainee's problem, then the trainer can assist the trainee in identifying a goal. If the trainee can relate his/her goal(s) to the training content, then he/she will have a reason to learn the training content.
Facts:	Personalization Trainee problems Trainer goals

Exercising Supportive Knowledge

See if you can develop the supportive knowledge leading to another training skill objective.

OBJECTIVE: _____

_____

_____

Skill Steps: _____

_____

_____

Supportive
Knowledge: _____

_____

_____

_____

_____

Repeat Exercise

Still another example of developing supportive knowledge might be the presentation of the supportive knowledge of an initial skill for a computer operator.

OBJECTIVE: The data processing trainee will initiate computer operations by inserting a floppy disk, right side up, into the disk drive unit to prepare it for data processing without damaging the disk at 99% accuracy when done repeatedly.

Skill Steps:
1. Open disk drive door.
2. Remove floppy disk from protective envelope.
3. Insert disk right side up into unit by following arrow on disk.
4. Close disk drive door.
5. If door does not close easily, remove disk and repeat Steps 3 and 4.

Principles: If the data processing trainee can insert a floppy disk into the disk drive, then he/she can prepare the drive to store and recall data so that he/she can successfully continue the data processing operations.

Concepts: If the trainee can open a disk drive door, then the trainee will be able to insert a floppy disk. If the trainee properly inserts the floppy disk into the unit, the disk drive door will close easily.

Facts: Floppy disk
Protective envelope
Disk drive
Disk drive door
Trainee

Exercising Supportive Knowledge

See if you can develop the supportive knowledge leading to a human resource development training skill objective.

OBJECTIVE: _____

_____

_____

_____

_____

Skill Steps: _____

_____

_____

_____

_____

Supportive
Knowledge: _____

_____

_____

_____

_____

Repeat Exercise

Another example of developing supportive knowledge is the soldering of wires in a computer terminal:

OBJECTIVE: The worker will solder wires in a computer terminal by soldering a 24-gauge wire to a terminal in such a way that the soldered connection is mechanically sound (holds together) and electronically sound (conducts electricity) as measured by the visual and written criteria.

Skill Steps: 1. Prepare materials.
2. Mechanically join wire to terminal.
3. Solder wire to terminal.
4. Inspect the connection.

Principles: If a solder connection is done correctly, then the worker will more efficiently and effectively join the wire to the terminal so that the assembly process is done within the stated quality and time performance standards.

Concepts: If the worker prepares his/her materials, then the soldering process can be accomplished most efficiently. If the worker understands the criteria of making a mechanically and electrically sound connection, then the worker will be able to know when a proper connection has been made.

Facts: Soldering iron
Solder
Flux pot
Wire cutters
24-gauge wire
Terminal

Exercising Supportive Knowledge

Now try to develop the supportive knowledge leading to still another technical training skill objective.

OBJECTIVE: _____

_____

_____

Skill Steps: _____

_____

_____

Supportive
Knowledge: _____

_____

_____

_____

_____

Repeat Exercise

You may wish to practice applying the use of supportive knowledge in your training specialty area. Try to make a variety of job-related applications. Also, try to make some applications to a home context or an educational context.

_____

_____

_____

_____

_____

Application Exercise

Summary

Perhaps you can again take some aspect of your training specialty and outline how you would develop your knowledge to support your skill step performance. This will give you an index of how well you learned your content.

_____

_____

_____

_____

_____

If you are able to develop your supportive knowledge effectively, then we have accomplished our training skill objective:

The instructional trainees will develop supportive knowledge for skill step performance by breaking the knowledge down into factual and conceptual levels under formal and informal conditions so that knowledge culminates into principles that can be transformed into training skill objectives.

Indexing Supportive Knowledge

If you have accomplished our training skill objective, then you should be confident of your ability to develop knowledge to support the achievement of the training skill objectives in your training specialty.

Facts:	The components, functions and processes to be used in the skill operation.
Concepts:	The relationships among the components, functions and processes to be used in the skill operation.
Principles:	The implications of the facts and concepts as they relate to the training skill objective.

Again, you will also be capable of "thinking on your feet" to fill in missing supportive knowledge in any training specialty. You may also wish to train your trainees how to develop supportive knowledge in order to prepare them for skill performance in their work.

LEVEL OF CONTENT
Skills
Skill Steps

SUPPORTIVE KNOWLEDGE
Facts
Concepts
Principles

Summarizing Supportive Knowledge

Now we have the facts, concepts and principles we need to support the training of our skill steps in our training specialty areas. Having such specialty areas to offer other human beings is what makes us unique as trainers and as humans. The concern for developing and transmitting skills and knowledge is what separates human beings from other forms of life. Developing our specialty areas is also what enables us to reach beyond our human experience. The development and convergence of different specialty areas makes movement from the known to the unknown possible. Humankind's goals in space or on Earth are limited only by the boundaries of our intellect. Hopefully, we will not forego our home on Earth prematurely. Hopefully, we will reach for the stars here on Earth.

References

American Management Association. *Training for Productivity*. Chicago, Ill.: American Management Association, 1980.

Berenson, D.H., Berenson, S.R. and Carkhuff, R.R. *The Skills of Teaching—Content Development Skills*. Amherst, Mass.: Human Resource Development Press, 1978.

Bloom, B. *Human Characteristics and School Learning*. New York: McGraw-Hill, 1982.

Brush, D.H. and Licata, B.J. "The Impact of Skill Learnability on the Effectiveness of Managerial Training Development." *Journal of Management*, 1983, 9, 27-39.

Carkhuff, R.R. *Sources of Human Productivity*. Amherst, Mass.: Human Resource Development Press, 1983.

Carkhuff, R.R. and Berenson, D.H. *The Skilled Teacher.* Amherst, Mass.: Human Resource Development Press, 1981.

Cenci, L. *Skill Training for the Job.* New York: Pitman Publishing, 1966.

Gagne, R.M. *Conditions of Learning.* New York: Holt, Rinehart and Winston, 1977.

Gilbert, T.F. *Praxeonomy: A Scientific Approach to Identifying Training Needs.* Ann Arbor, Mich.: University of Michigan Graduate School of Business, 1978.

Kaya, E., Gerhard, M., Staslewski, A. and Berenson, D.H. *Developing a Theory of Educational Practices at the Elementary School.* Norwalk, Conn.: Ford Foundation Fund for the Improvement of Education, 1967.

Mager, R.F. *Preparing Instructional Objectives.* San Francisco, Calif.: Fearon Publishers, 1962.

Mallory, W.A. "A Task Analytic Approach to Specifying Technical Training Needs." *Training and Development Journal,* 1982, *36,* 66-68.

Martin, A. "Management Training in British Telecommunications." *Personnel Management,* 1982, *14,* 52.

Moscowitz, R.A. *How to Increase Learning Effectiveness.* Chicago, Ill.: American Management Association, 1982.

Odiorne, G. *Training by Objectives.* Marshfield, Mass.: Pitman Press, 1965.

Ryle, G. *Concept of Mind.* New York: Barnes and Noble, 1949.

IV

PREPARING THE TRAINING DELIVERY

With the content in hand, we are ready to plan the training delivery. The training delivery plan emphasizes two essential factors: 1) organizing the content; and 2) developing the training methods. The content organization and training methods interact with each other in guiding the delivery of the training content. They dictate the level of skills delivered as well as the roles of trainers and trainees in implementing the delivery.

CONTENT ORGANIZATION

TRAINING METHODS	Review	Overview	Present	Exercise	Summarize
Tell					
Show					
Do					

7

Organizing the Training Content

Our training delivery is to our training preparation as marketing is to product development. We have developed our product—our content. We must now plan to market that content to our trainees. Planning for our marketing campaign does not have to be a dreary activity. It is ever bit as exciting as planning for a ball game or a theatrical presentation. We must plan our training delivery with the same care and detail with which we developed our content. We plan first by organizing content for delivery. We also plan by developing the methods of delivery. We will implement our plan by using our training delivery skills. We are very fortunate in developing our marketing plan. We believe in our product. The challenge of marketing is to deliver the product in such a way that other people will come to believe in it too.

Review and Overview

All content requires an organization that reflects its purpose (Carkhuff and Berenson, 1981; Novak, 1977). In other words, the content must be organized sequentially in order to achieve its purpose: making a skill application (Berenson, Berenson and Carkhuff, 1978; Gagne, 1977; Mager, 1968). Training in skill applications is done by assessing the preparedness of the trainees for the training, introducing the goals of the content, presenting the mechanics of the content, and practicing the skills. Overall, the research indicates that trainers who organize their content in ways meaningful for the trainees are most effective (Bloom, 1982; Blumenthal, 1977; Bronson, 1975; Flanders, 1965; Nadler, 1982; Resnick, 1981; Ribler, 1983). In the Program on Teaching Effectiveness (1976), the teachers' "structuring" activities consist of the following: reviewing the main ideas covered in the lesson; stating objectives at the beginning of the lesson; indicating the important points in a lesson; and summarizing the parts of the lesson as the lesson proceeded. Giving learners additional time to exercise the skill steps results in anticipated increases in skills and knowledge (American Educational Research Association, 1966; Killian, 1978; McCullough, 1963; Moscowitz, 1982) independent of kinds of materials and methods used. Also, increasing the time spent on learning tasks increases skill learning (Bloom, 1982; Gardner, 1982).

Principles of Organizing Content

The training skill objective of this lesson is as follows:

The instructional trainees will organize content for their training delivery by sequencing the phases of our skill delivery under formal and informal conditions with instructional trainees able to organize their training to maximize trainee skill applications.

Before you learn to organize your content, you may want an index of your skills in this area. Perhaps you can organize your training specialty content for a training delivery. Outline how you would organize the content in achievable terms:

_____

_____

_____

_____

_____

Indexing Organization of Content

You did well if you emphasized the trainer's presentation and the trainee's exercises of the skills and knowledge. The effective ingredients of organizing emphasize Reviewing, Overviewing, Presenting, Exercising and Summarizing the content (ROPES).

REVIEWING the content to obtain a picture of the trainees' abilities before the training.

OVERVIEWING the content to match our images of the content and its importance with those of the trainees.

PRESENTING the content to deliver our skills and knowledge to the trainees.

EXERCISING the content to provide the trainees with opportunities to practice the skills.

SUMMARIZING the content to provide the trainees with a follow-up picture of their skill abilities after training.

A trainer quickly realizes that all of these ingredients are needed in various combinations with the skills, skill steps and supportive knowledge of one's training specialty. You want to insure your delivery to the trainees. Most important you want to insure the trainee's reception of the content. To this end, you will want to organize the training content in a ROPES framework that will facilitate the trainee's reception of the content.

CONTENT ORGANIZATION

Review • Overview • Present • Exercise • Summarize

Overviewing Organization of Content

Reviewing

Before we train our trainees in a new skill, we need to review what skills and knowledge our trainees need and compare it to what the trainees actually have. We must ask the question, "What other skills do our trainees need to have before they can perform the new skill?" The review provides us with an answer to this question. The review allows us to know where our trainees are in relation to the content we are about to deliver. Sometimes the review is a very illuminating training experience because we find out our trainees can perform many related skills and recall much supportive knowledge. At times the review is a very distressing experience because we find just how little the trainees know and can perform. At all times, we find that our trainees' performances are reflections of how well they have been trained previously. After all, except for the beginning of a new training program, we have taught our trainees what they can perform. The review gives both trainer and trainee the opportunity to explore where they are in relation to the content to be learned.

REVIEW: Contingency Skills
and
Supportive Knowledge

Reviewing

The review gives us an opportunity to gauge the trainees' level of functioning on contingency skills, or skills that are required in order to perform the current skill to be acquired. For example, in order to write a correct sentence, our trainees must be able to write, spell and identify the subject and predicate, among other things. In order for trainees to establish rapport in a telemarketing call they must be able to dial the phone, get the sales prospect on the phone, and properly identify themselves, among other things. When we review, we are making a determination of where the trainees are in relation to the new skill they are about to acquire. The essential learning for a trainer at this point is in identifying what the trainees can already do, what they already know and how the trainees feel about the training skill objective. For example, in reviewing contingency skills related to training sales personnel in interpersonal communication skills, we may develop a review as our entry training experience. We might ask the sales personnel trainee to persuade the other trainees to take some action then take an index as to that trainee's use of each of the major interpersonal skills steps, i.e., getting the other perspective, giving your own perspective, merging differences, and going on to action.

REVIEW: Contingency Skills

Training
Tasks: 1. Give trainees persuasion assignment.
2. Take index of trainees' skills.
3. Discuss results with trainees.

Reviewing Contingency Skills

The trainees may be surprised by their difficulty in persuading others to take action. Such review steps will yield an index of the trainees' abilities to perform the skill steps involved. In addition, a discussion of the skill steps will yield an index of the level of supportive knowledge which the trainees have relative to the skill. At this point you may find it helpful to list the training tasks in which you would involve your trainees when reviewing your training specialty content. Remember, the fundamental purpose of the review is to develop a training experience which provides a diagnosis of the trainees' levels of functioning in the skills and knowledge of your content. The nature of that training should be as varied, unique and creative as possible.

REVIEW: Contingency Skills

Training
Tasks: 1. _____

2. _____

3. _____

Practicing Reviewing

Overviewing

Once we have a picture of where the trainees are, we need to develop an overview of where they want or need to be. This is a very exciting part of organizing content because we get to share our training goals with the trainees. The overview can also be stimulating because it gives the trainees an opportunity to share their images of the training goals. The overview, then, provides both trainer and trainees with a chance to relate their images of the skills and their applications. By relating images, the trainees compare their experiences relative to the training goals with those of the trainer. At the same time the trainers can compare their training goals with the trainees' experiences of the trainers. We overview a new skill to reach a consensus with the trainees about the reason for acquiring the skill. The primary purpose a trainer uses to motivate trainees should be the application of the skill to the trainees' job tasks. The skill applications and knowledge demonstrated by the trainer will illustrate the trainer's extensive repertoire of responses. The trainer must show competency when illustrating applications relevant to the trainees. In short, the trainer must do it better. The net effect of this image comparison is the facilitation of the trainees' understanding of where they are in relation to where they want to be.

> **OVERVIEW:**   Skill Applications
> and
> Supportive Knowledge

Overviewing

Inventory control trainers may make the rapid calculations to determine the replacement number of a depleted inventory item or in predicting the amount of time before an inventory item will be out of stock. Plastics injection mold operation trainers may demonstrate the ability to run the injection mold at high speeds. Then, instead of saying "We know we can do that," the trainees will say, "Train us so that we can do that." In overviewing the skill applications training sales personnel how to communicate interpersonally with customers, we can develop an overview of the skills to be acquired. We do this by developing the potential skill applications and relating them to the skills to be acquired through the development of principles.

OVERVIEW: Skill Applications

Principles: If you learn to communicate interpersonally with customers, then you can better understand their point of view and give yours so that your chances of serving them and persuading them are increased.

Training
Experiences: 1. Show a videotaped excerpt of a Customer Service Representative (CSR) with good interpersonal communication skills.
2. Discuss with trainees the strengths and weaknesses of the way in which the CSR handles the customer.

Overviewing Skill Applications

This overview can be a very dramatic illustration of a skill application. It is also directly relevant to real-life applications. The salespeople will find that the more they communicate interpersonally with customers, the more customers will express themselves. At this point you may want to list the skill applications relevant to the trainees' functioning more effectively in their work settings. Then, develop one or more training experiences to demonstrate the skill applications.

OVERVIEW: Skill Applications

Principles: _____

_____

_____

Training
Experiences: 1. _____

_____

2. _____

_____

3. _____

_____

Practicing Overviewing

Presenting

Once the trainees know what the training skill objectives are we need to present the steps to achieve them. When we present, we teach our trainees how to perform a skill. The presentation is the "how to do it" part of organizing content. The presentation is the most involved part of content organization and also provides us an opportunity to demonstrate our expertise. It is our expertise that makes us trainers and its demonstration that makes us credible. Our moments of presentation give us our pride in our skills and knowledge of a specialty area and our ability to deliver them. In order to prepare our presentation, we must break down the skill steps our trainees need to do in order to perform the skill. This is the most critical part of our planning. In effect, this means breaking the skills into trainee-sized steps.

> **PRESENT:**   Skill Steps
> and
> Supportive Knowledge

New employees often ask, "What do I do first?" "What do I do next?" What they are really asking for are the discrete steps and knowledge they need to successfully perform the skill. What we do is break down the skill into the steps trainees require. For example, when instructing trainees to tighten a nut, we might break the skill steps down as follows:

1. Place the socket wrench over the nut.
2. Turn socket wrench clockwise until you cannot turn it anymore with that hand.
3. Turn socket wrench counterclockwise until it is in its original starting position.
4. Repeat Steps 3 and 4 until socket wrench will not turn clockwise.
5. Remove socket wrench from nut.

If the skill steps are incomplete, the chances are that the trainees will be unsuccessful. One way of checking the steps is for us to actually perform what we have written.

Presenting Steps

For example, in presenting sales personnel with the skill steps of interpersonal communication, we may break down the skill steps to include all the skill substeps necessary for their performance.

PRESENT: Interpersonal Communications Skill Steps.

Objective: The Customer Service Representatives (CSRs) will communicate whenever interacting with customers, by getting the customer's perspective, giving her (or his) own perspective, merging any differences and going on to action at such a level that the customer will feel served.

Skill Steps: 1. Get the customer's perspective.
2. Give your own perspective.
3. Merge any differences in perspectives.
4. Go on to action.

Supportive Knowledge:
Principles: 1. If the CSR gets the customer's perspective, then she (or he) will understand the customer so that the CSR has the information needed to serve or persuade the customer.
2. If the CSR gives the customer her (or his) perspective, then the customer will have additional information so that the customer is better served.

Example of Presenting Skill Steps

3. If the CSR works to merge any differences in perspectives, then action will
be taken that meets the customer's
needs so that the opportunity for
repeat business is enhanced.

4. If the CSR develops a specific action
plan for the customer, then the planned action can be monitored so that
the CSR insures the customer is
served.

Concepts: 1. If the CSR gets the customer's
perspective, then she (or he) will
understand the customer.

2. If the CSR gives the customer her (or
his) perspective, then the customer
will have additional information.

3. If the CSR works to merge any differences in perspectives, then action will
be taken that meets the customer's
needs.

4. If the CSR develops a specific plan of
action for the customer, then the
planned action can be monitored.

Facts: Attending physically, observing, listening, reflecting, specifics, genuineness,
respect, goals, values, integrative solutions, compromise solutions, accom-
modation, action plan.

Example of Presenting Skill Steps

The trainees should find all of the steps and knowledge they require to achieve the training skill objective. The steps should be so small or simple as to seem absurd. This atomistic simplicity insures trainee acquisition. The presentation trains the trainees the skill steps required for them to get from where they are to where they want to be. At this point you may want to define your training skill objective and list your skill steps and supportive knowledge in your training specialty. You should be able to draw from the content you have already developed to perform these tasks.

PRESENT: _____

Objective: _____

_____

Skill Steps: 1. _____

2. _____

3. _____

Supportive
Knowledge:
Principles: _____

Concepts: _____

Facts: _____

_____

Practicing Presenting

Exercising

Now that the skill steps have been presented, the trainees need an opportunity to practice them. The exercise is really an opportunity for the trainees to "own" the skill. By practicing the skill over and over, or by being exposed to individually designed training experiences, the trainees acquire the skill and have it available for appropriate applications in their work settings. Exercising does not introduce any new content. Instead, it involves the trainees in repeated use of the skill. It also provides the opportunity for the trainer to "shape" the skills and skill steps by repeating the instructions that were presented. Ideally, the exercising will follow a sequence. First the skill is performed by itself. Then the trainees will be required to do exercises that use the skill in conjunction with other skills. Exercising facilitates the trainees' reception and incorporation of the skills into their repertoires of work skills. It serves to reinforce the action steps needed to get the trainees from where they are to where they want to be.

EXERCISE: Skill Steps

Exercising

The more times we can involve the trainees in using a new skill, the more we increase their chances of being able to master it. A variety of practice materials and applications keep the training exciting. For example, in a simple exercise for using the skills of operating a socket wrench, the trainer may use different kinds of nuts, different placements of nuts and bolts, tightening nuts, loosening nuts, etc. In addition, the trainer might develop a variety of exercises around different skill applications incorporating the skills: inserting and extracting spark plugs, attaching metal sheeting, building steel frame supports, dismantling an appliance, etc. For example, in developing practice exercises for our sales personnel to practice interpersonal communication, we may vary both the learning experiences (customers and products) and the skill applications (individual customers, a group of customers). In addition we can develop exercises that incorporate other skills, such as handling complaints.

EXERCISE: Interpersonal Communications Skill Steps

Training
Experiences:
1. With an eager customer.
2. With a resistant customer.
3. With an angry customer.
4. With a group of customers with mixed reactions.
5. With a customer who has a product complaint.

Exercising Skill Steps

These exercises will give the trainees a familiarity with the use of interpersonal communication skills in a variety of different customer situations. The more variable the skill applications, the greater their generalizability or transferability. The more integrated they are with other skills, the more natural and useful will be their application. You may now want to practice developing exercises for practicing skill steps. You should try to vary both the training materials and the skill applications. Also, you will want to incorporate other skills that the trainees have mastered, if appropriate.

EXERCISE: _____

Training
Experiences: 1. _____

2. _____

3. _____

4. _____

5. _____

Practicing Exercising

Summarizing

After we teach our trainees the skill steps, we must summarize their learnings. Summarizing answers the question: "What have the trainees learned?" The summary provides an opportunity to assess where the trainees are after the training. Just as the initial review assessed contingency skills, the summary assessed trainee skill acquisition as a result of the training. The summary is an index of our training as well as the trainees' learning. It stimulates a recycling of the training process of exploring, understanding and acting. What the summary really does is give the trainer the opportunity to review the new skill and knowledge with the trainees. Summarizing, then, serves the same function as reviewing—assessing trainee skill performance.

SUMMARIZE: Skill Performance
and
Supportive Knowledge

Summarizing

The summary lets us diagnose where our trainees are in relation to what we trained. Most important, the summary provides the trainees with the opportunity to diagnose themselves in relation to the content they have acquired. Thus, trainees may summarize the steps of performing the skill. We can diagnose where the trainees are in relation to what has been trained. One way to develop the summary is to provide a training experience, such as we initially did in the review. Having the trainees develop their own summary experience is an acceptable alternate strategy.

SUMMARIZE: Interpersonal Communication Skill Performance

Training Tasks:
1. Have sales personnel trainee relate to a customer in a simulated sales situation.
2. Have sales personnel trainee evaluate her (or his) effectiveness in communicating with the "customer."
3. Have sales personnel trainee discuss the skill steps involved in relating to customers.

Summarizing Skills

Hopefully, the trainees will not be as surprised by their ability to communicate with customers this time. They should know what the dimensions of communicating with customers are. They should be applying these dimensions on the sales floor as well as in other experiences. They should be using those skills to get the customer's perspective, give their perspective, merge any differences in perspectives and go on to action. Such summary steps will yield an index of what the trainees have learned, in terms of both knowledge and skills. At this point, you may want to list the training tasks in which you would involve your trainees in summarizing the training content. Remember, the fundamental purpose of the summary is to develop a training experience which provides a diagnosis of the trainees' levels of functioning in the skills and knowledge of your content.

SUMMARIZE: _____

Training
Tasks: 1. _____

2. _____

3. _____

Practicing Summarizing

Exercises

We can apply the ROPES method of content organization in all areas of life. We can use it to organize new information when "thinking on our feet," in or out of training. We can also use it to meet large or small training objectives. We can apply ROPES in any critical situation that involves training and learning. For example, we could employ ROPES for organizing content in communicating with professional colleagues, at home with our families, or with friends. We could also use ROPES when communicating in order to develop human resources with subordinates or even superiors at work. This process is illustrated below:

OBJECTIVE: The second-level managers will develop human resources by leading first-level supervisors through a group goal-setting process in such a way that clear measures of successful problem resolution are established.

Content Organization:

Review: Illustrating and assessing use of observation, listening and indirect data collection processes.

Overview: Demonstrating an application of establishing a clearly measurable goal and its impact in a problem-solving process.

Present: Delivering the skills and skill steps of group goal-setting.

Exercise: Practicing group goal-setting skill steps with repeat-and-apply exercises.

Summarize: Summarizing skills of group goal-setting and assessing the managers' skills acquisition.

Exercising Organization of Content

Try to organize your training content to achieve an important human resource development training skill objective.

OBJECTIVE: _____

_____

_____

Content
Organization:
Review: _____

_____

Overview: _____

_____

Present: _____

_____

Exercise: _____

_____

Summarize: _____

_____

Repeat Exercise

The ROPES method can be used for highly complex information resource development.

OBJECTIVE: The internal medicine resident will make a tentative diagnosis of metastatic or infiltrative disease of the liver by correctly interpreting the following laboratory test results: serum bilirubin, urine bilirubin, serum leucine aminopeptiduse (LAP), serum alkaline phosphatase, glutamic oxalacetic, transaminase, glutamic pyravic transaminase, 5' neucleotidase, isocitric dehydrogenase, a bromxulphalein retention test, as well as radioactive scanning of the liver and a blink needle biopsy. This diagnosis will occur within one hour of receiving the test results using the criteria established by the interpretation of diagnostic tests.

Exercising Organization of Content

Content
Organization:

Review: Illustrating the tests to be used, what they measure, and how to generally use the results for interpretation.

Overview: Demonstrating metastatic and in-filtrative liver disease and their effects.

Present: Delivering the skills and skill steps of conducting and interpreting the recommended clinical tests for diagnosis of metastatic or infiltrative liver disease.

Exercise: Practicing skill steps of conducting and interpreting clinical tests for diagnoses by repeat-and-apply exercises.

Summarize: Reviewing the skills of interpreting clinical tests for diagnosis of metastatic or infiltrative liver disease and assessing the resident's skills acquisition.

Exercising Organization of Content

Now try to organize your training content to achieve another important training skill objective.

OBJECTIVE: _____

_____

_____

Content
Organization:
Review: _____

_____

Overview: _____

_____

Present: _____

_____

Exercise: _____

_____

Summarize: _____

_____

Repeat Exercise

ROPES can be used for training to achieve any kind of technical training skill objective.

OBJECTIVE: The word processing trainee will "log-on" to the computer system as measured by the response on the computer CRT of the word HELLO.

Content Organization:

Review: Discussing and assessing the trainee's knowledge of the terminal keyboard functions as well as how to turn on the terminal.

Overview: Illustrating how proper "log-on" skills will allow the trainee to utilize all of the computer programs as learning and working tools.

Present: Delivering the skills for "logging-on".

Exercise: Practicing skill steps for "logging-on".

Summarize: Reviewing the skills of "logging-on" and assessing the trainee's acquisition of "log-on" skills.

Exercising Organization of Content

Now try to organize your training content to achieve a technical training skill objective.

OBJECTIVE: _____

_____

_____

Content
Organization:
Review: _____

_____

Overview: _____

_____

Present: _____

_____

Exercise: _____

_____

Summarize: _____

_____

Repeat Exercise

You may wish to practice applying the use of ROPES in your training specialty area. Try to make a variety of job-related applications of ROPES. Also, try to make some applications to a home context or an educational context.

_____

_____

_____

_____

_____

Application Exercise

Summary
Perhaps you can now organize your content to achieve your training skill objective in your training specialty. Simply outline how you would organize the content in achievable terms:

_____

_____

_____

_____

_____

If you are able to organize your content effectively, then we have accomplished our training skill objective:

The instructional trainees will organize content for their training delivery by sequencing the phases of our skill delivery under formal and informal conditions with instructional trainees able to organize their training to maximize trainee skill applications.

Indexing Content Organization

If you have accomplished the training skill objective, then you are capable of productively organizing your content to achieve your training skill objectives in your specialty.

REVIEWING:	Contingency Skill Performance
OVERVIEWING:	Skill Applications
PRESENTING:	Skill Steps
EXERCISING:	Skill Steps
SUMMARIZING:	Skill Performance

You will also be capable of "thinking on your feet" to organize your content in any communication, formal or informal. You may also wish to involve your trainees in learning the ROPES method of organizing content in order to prepare them for communicating their future content to others.

CONTENT ORGANIZATION

REVIEW SKILLS	•	OVERVIEW SKILLS	•	PRESENT SKILL STEPS	•	EXERCISE SKILL STEPS	•	SUMMARIZE SKILLS

Summarizing Organization of Content

The ROPES approach of organizing content is itself related to the natural movement of trainees through the training process: exploring where they are, understanding where they want to be, acting to get to their goals. Perhaps this is the most important contribution of content organizing skills: to facilitate the trainees' cycling and recycling of the phases of training. In this respect, the ROPES organization is attached to the most precious and fragile process of humankind: learning to become human through the transmission of the skills and knowledge which make us human. The trainer is a central factor in the transmission of these humanizing skills from one generation to the next. And the content of the delivery plan is organized to facilitate the transmission of these skills.

References

American Educational Research Association. *Review of Educational Research*. Washington, D.C.: American Educational Research Association, 1966.

Berenson, D.H., Berenson, S.R. and Carkhuff, R.R. *The Skills of Teaching—Lesson Planning Skills*. Amherst, Mass.: Human Resource Development Press, 1981.

Bloom, B.J. *Human Characteristics and School Learning*. New York: McGraw-Hill, 1982.

Blumenthal, A. *The Process of Cognition*. Englewood Cliffs, N.J.: Prentice-Hall, 1977.

Bronson, R.K. *Inservice Procedures for Instructional Systems Development*. Tallahassee, Fla.: Center for Educational Technology, 1975.

Carkhuff, R.R. and Berenson, D.H. *The Skilled Teacher*. Amherst, Mass.: Human Resource Development Press, 1981.

Flanders, N.A. *Teacher Influence, Pupil Attitudes and Achievement*. Washington, D.C.: HEW, 1965.

Gagne, R.M. *Conditions of Learning*. New York: Holt, Rinehart and Winston, 1977.

Gardner, J.E. *Training Interventions in Job Skill Development*. Reading, Mass.: Addison-Wesley, 1981.

Killian, R.A. "Developing Full Performance and Potential." Chapter in *Human Resource Development*. Chicago, Ill.: American Management Association, 1978.

Mager, R.F. *Developing Attitude Toward Learning*. San Francisco, Calif.: Fearon Publishers, 1968.

McCullough, C.M. "What Does Research Reveal About Practices in Teaching Reading?" In N.L. Gage (Ed.), *Handbook of Research on Teaching*. Chicago, Ill.: Rand McNally, 1963.

Moscowitz, R.A. *How to Increase Learning Effectiveness*. Chicago, Ill.: American Management Association, 1982.

Nadler, L. *Designing Training Programs*. Reading, Mass.: Addison-Wesley, 1982.

Novak, J. *A Theory of Education*. Ithaca, N.Y.: Cornell University Press, 1977.

Program on Teaching Effectiveness, SCRDT. Stanford, Calif.: Stanford Center for Research and Development in Teaching, 1976.

Resnick, L.B. "Instructional Psychology." In M.P. Rosenzweig and L.W. Porter (Eds.). *Annual Review of Psychology*, 1981, *32*, 659-704.

Ribler, R. *Training Development Guide*. Reston, Va.: Reston Publishing Co., 1983.

8

Developing the Training Methods

Typically, when trainers think of training methods, they think of certain training orientations and materials like classroom instruction or computer-assisted instruction or self-instructional materials. These orientations are, to be sure, vehicles for presenting methods. However, the methods within these vehicles may vary widely. In fact, there are as many different kinds of training methods as there are trainers. Unfortunately, most trainers emphasize one or two training methods to the exclusion of others. There is a "variety principle" that characterizes effective training methods: the more methods the trainer employs, the more effective is the training; the more different ways the trainer involves the trainees, the more skill acquisition takes place. Thus, the principle of variety carries with it the criterion of participation.

Review and Overview

The primary sources of learning are fourfold: didactic, modeling, experiential and shaping (Carkhuff, 1971, 1981; Carkhuff and Berenson, 1981). Our training methods are derived directly from these sources of learning. In didactic training, we teach all of those things that enable the trainee to perform the skill. In modeling, we train by behaving and doing while being observed. In experiential training, we provide others the opportunity to perform the skill. In shaping, we provide feedback for the trainee's skill performance. In general, research indicates that trainees acquire skills differently according to the training methods emphasized. "You get what you emphasize in training," i.e., knowledge from lectures and skills from experiential exercises (Dubin and Taveggia, 1968; Gage, 1976, 1977; Kolb, 1976; McKeachie and Kulik, 1975; Nadler, 1982; Neidler, 1981). In other words, trainees learn best what they spend the most time doing. In this context, trainers who employ a variety of methods are effective (Bloom, 1981; Carkhuff and Berenson, 1981; Engel, 1973; Howe, 1980; Laird, 1982). When these methods, in turn, utilize the different sensory modalities, especially kinesthetic experiences, they are effective.

Principles of Training Methods

One training skill objective in this lesson is as follows:

The instructional trainees will develop training methods by employing various sensory modalities under formal and informal conditions with instructional trainees able to develop training methods to maximize trainee skill applications.

Before you learn to develop your methods, you may want an index of your skills in this area. Perhaps you can develop methods for your training specialty. Outline how you would develop the training methods in achievable terms.

_____

_____

_____

_____

_____

Indexing Training Methods

You did well if you emphasized the trainees' various sensory modalities: hearing, seeing, doing. The effective ingredients of developing training methods emphasize *telling*, *showing*, and *doing*.

TELLING the trainees what skills to do and how to do them.
SHOWING the trainees how to do the skills.
DOING by providing the trainees opportunities to do the skills.

We will realize that we need all of these methods in combination with the skills and skill steps in order to ensure our delivery and the trainees' reception of the skills. To this end, we will develop our training methods by a *Tell-Show-Do* format that will facilitate the trainees' reception of the content.

TRAINING METHODS
Tell
Show
Do

Overviewing Training Methods

Telling

Telling is the most common training method. For most trainers, the easiest way to deliver skills is to tell the trainees what they need to know and do. Because it appears to be the easiest method requiring the least energy, trainers are most comfortable with this mode. *Tell* methods answer the question, "What am I going to use to tell my trainees what they want to learn?"

   Tell methods are essential but not sufficient for the training delivery. We *tell* the trainees about new training content. If they need a fact like a name of an object, we identify the object—for example, "an internal combustion engine." If the trainees need a concept like the concept of compression: "If a piston moves up in the cylinder, then the fuel and air mixture is squeezed into a smaller space. This is compression." In a like manner, we will tell trainees about the principle involved. "If a piston moves up in the cylinder, then the fuel and air mixture is squeezed into a smaller space so that combustion can take place with adequate force." Similarly, telling trainees how to perform the steps of a skill could include the following: "The first step is to check the spark plugs to see if they need cleaning or replacement."

Tell methods emphasize dealing with words, either spoken or written. You can increase your variety of *tell* methods by varying the source of the explanation, e.g., trainer, trainee, guest speaker or videotaped expert. You can increase the variety of your *tell* methods by varying the procedure used, e.g., lecture, discussion, question and answer. Finally, you can increase your *tell* methods by varying the equipment and materials you use, e.g., overhead projector, flip chart, handouts. For example, you might take a basic *tell* procedure such as group discussion and vary the source of the explanation, e.g., an instructor-lead discussion or a trainee-lead discussion. You can add further variety with equipment and materials, e.g., record discussion results on a flip chart or record them on a transparency.

Telling Methods

For example, we can use *tell* methods in implementing our presentation of the first skill step to sales personnel, getting the customer's perspective.

	PRESENTATION
OBJECTIVE:	Customer Service Representatives (CSRs) will communicate interpersonally by getting the customer's perspective, communicating their own perspective, merging differences and going to action, in all customer contacts, at a level that insures the customer is heard and feels served.
Skill Step #1:	Get customer's perspective.
Tell Methods:	Trainer assigns small group leaders to build a list on newsprint of the steps involved in getting a customer's perspective. Trainer then lectures in the following skill substeps, integrating the trainee's material.

Get customer's perspective

Reflecting the customer's feelings and stated content

Listening to the customer

Observing the customer

Attending physically

Example of Telling

The *tell* methods should detail the skill steps leading toward achievement of the training skill objective. The trainees should find all of the steps they will need in their mostly auditory reception of the words contained in the *tell* method. They should find out what they are going to do and how to do it. At this point, you may find it helpful to select a training skill objective and list the first skill step. Then indicate at least one *tell* method that you might employ to orient the trainees to the training tasks.

OBJECTIVE: _____

Skill Step #1: _____

Tell Methods: _____

_____

_____

_____

_____

Practicing Telling

Showing

An extremely potent source of training is *showing*. Yet, we are most uncomfortable about *showing*, because we think it takes great energy and sometimes puts us "on the spot." *Showing* is a critical training method because it visually demonstrates the skill to be performed. The trainees have the opportunity to observe the steps involved in the skills demonstration. They have the meaning of the words through *telling*, and the demonstration of skills through *showing*, to guide them toward their skills performance. When we *tell* trainees something is called an "internal combustion engine," we should also *show* them what an engine looks like. Before we *tell* trainees about compression, we may want to *show* them what happens when gas is compressed. Our *show* method visually explains the principle trainees need to understand—the compression cycle of the engine. We also *tell* and *show* the steps of performing the skills. When we *tell* the trainees to check the spark plug, we need to *show* them how to do so at the same time.

Showing

While *tell* methods deal with words, *show* methods deal with pictures. The trainees develop mental pictures from the descriptive words we use, or from the pictures we exhibit. The proverb, "A picture is worth a thousand words," is a popular statement of the principle which accounts for the effectiveness of *show* methods, especially for visual learners. The *show* methods deliver to the trainees a picture, a diagram, a series of pictures or the action of performing the skills. The most common *show* method is the demonstration in which the trainer shows the skill steps to the trainee. For example, we may want to teach our trainees how to splice a solid core electric wire. We might *tell* them how to do it and *show* them how to do it. We might ask trainees who already have the skill to demonstrate. We could use films, slides, pictures, overhead projectors, posters, models, or computer graphics to train the skills with a series of pictures. We can use any one or several of these methods as *show* methods. As with *tell* methods, the variety of *show* methods can be increased by varying the combinations of the source of the illustrations, the procedures used and the equipment or materials.

Showing Methods

For example, we can use *show* methods in implementing our presentation of the first skill step, getting the customer's perspective:

PRESENTATION

OBJECTIVE: Customer Service Representatives (CSRs) will communicate interpersonally by getting the customer's perspective, communicating their own perspective, merging differences and going to action, in all customer contacts, at a level that insures the customer is heard and feels served.

Skill Step #1: Get customer's perspective.
Show Methods: Trainer demonstrates the skill substeps of getting perspective, using one of the trainees role playing the part of the customer.

Example of Showing

The *show* methods should provide pictures of the training skill objective and the steps needed to achieve it. The trainees should obtain all of the pictures they require from their visual reception of the *show* method. They should have complete pictures of what they are going to do and how to do it.

Now, develop at least one *show* method that you might employ to provide your trainees with pictures of their skill tasks:

OBJECTIVE: _____

Skill Step #1: _____

Show Methods: _____

_____

_____

_____

_____

Practicing Showing

Doing

The most potent source of skill acquisition is *doing*. The purpose of the *do* method is to provide trainees with the opportunity to experience the skills by doing them. *Do* methods actually involve the trainees in the performance of the skills. Often, while trainers are comfortable with their trainers doing work assignments, they do not understand how to use this method for its full potency. *Do* methods are actually training experiences that the trainer designs to have trainees participate in or perform the training tasks. The trainer may also use training experiences when new words and definitions are introduced. Planning activities which have the trainees use facts and concepts will involve them in writing, speaking or drawing. For example, a laboratory that allows trainees to identify bacteria in a water sample should allow trainees to manipulate the water sample as well as the testing equipment. The trainees actually perform the skill of making a bacteria count while learning the supportive knowledge.

We are all kinesthetic learners. While some of us have audio or visual preferences, we all learn by doing. We file permanent images of our behavior when we *do* the skills. We provide trainees with a kinesthetic learning experience when we have each trainee perform the skills. The nature of the skills will determine which *do* methods are most appropriate. The most common *do* method is the worksheet. It provides the trainer with an opportunity to measure the trainees' correct responses. However, many skills cannot be performed on a worksheet because the answers only describe the skill. For example, we may want to teach trainees how to buff a metal finish. After we have told and shown, we will want to plan an activity that requires everyone to *do* the skill. This means that we will have to provide each trainee with an opportunity to buff a metal finish. While the trainees, by definition, must always be involved in performing a *do* method, variety can be increased through using different procedures, e.g., case studies, role plays, simulations, questionnaires and different equipment/materials, e.g., worksheets, audiotapes, videotapes.

Doing Methods

Providing trainees with an opportunity to *do* the skills, then, is the next step in our sequence of training methods. Doing gives our trainees the opportunity for a "hands-on" experience of the skills. In implementing the delivery plan, our *do* methods address every step of content organization just as our *tell* and *show* methods. *Tell*, *show* and *do* methods implement all steps of our ROPES delivery plan. For example, we can use *do* methods in implementing our presentation of the first skill step when training sales personnel to get the customer's perspective.

PRESENTATION

OBJECTIVE: Customer Service Representatives (CSRs) will communicate interpersonally by getting the customer's perspective, communicating their own perspective, merging differences and going to action, in all customer contacts, at a level that insures the customer is heard and feels served.

Skill Step #1: Get customer's perspective.
Do Methods: Two trainees role play the skills of getting the customer's perspective in front of the group. The interaction is taped and feedback is given. Continue the process until all trainees have had an opportunity to do the getting perspective skill step.

Example of Doing

The *do* methods should provide the trainees with the experience of performing the skills. The trainees should have a complete experience of doing the skills. Now, develop at least one *do* method that you might employ to provide your trainees with the experience of performing the skill:

OBJECTIVE: _____

Skill Step #1: _____

Do Methods: _____

_____

_____

_____

_____

How many other *do* methods can you think of to help your trainees experience doing the skills?

Practicing Doing

Repeating

Doing demonstrates skill acquisition. *Repeating* insures skill acquisition. *Repeat* methods are just what the label suggests: methods which repeat the skill steps. They involve practice exercises that enable the trainees to retain the skill through repetition. While trainers are usually comfortable with their trainees' being occupied in doing practice exercises, use of the exercises is often more for the trainers' benefit than that of the trainees. It is necessary for the trainee to repeat the skill by her or himself. This way trainees can concentrate upon performing the new skill's steps. One illustration of a way to plan the *repeat* exercises is to organize a performance competition among the trainees. For example, if you want trainees to learn how to paint decorative trim, some methods that could be used for repeat exercises include varying shape of the objects, having accuracy contests among trainees, having speed contests among trainees, or having consistency contests among trainees. In this manner the trainees are repeating only one skill. It would not be appropriate to have them create their own trim designs at this time. If they did, they would have to use other skills such as organizing layout and making color choices.

Repeating is really the trainees' *tell-show-do*. The trainers told and showed the trainees' what to do and how to do it. The trainers provided trainees with the opportunity to do it. In *repeating* the skill, trainees have the opportunity to *tell-show-do* their own learning experience. While they are performing the skill (*do*), they present a description (*tell*) and the pictures (*show*) concerning the performance of the skill. Once *repeat* methods are selected for the exercise, we can consider ways trainees will *repeat* the skill within these methods. It would not be sufficient practice for the trainees to paint the trim on one piece of furniture, or make a decorative scroll once. We must expand the repetitions within the method as carefully as we selected the method. As with *do* methods, *repeat* methods can be increased by varying the procedures, equipment and materials.

Repeating Methods

Providing trainees with an opportunity to *repeat* the skills is the next step in our sequence of training methods. *Repeating* gives trainees the opportunity to practice the skills. In implementing the delivery plan, *repeat* methods address only the "exercise" step of content organization. The *repeat* methods follow the *tell-show-do* methods only during the exercise of the skills. For example, we can use *repeat* methods in implementing our presentation of the first skill step when training sales personnel in interpersonal communication skills.

PRESENTATION

OBJECTIVE: Customer Service Representatives (CSRs) will communicate interpersonally by getting the customer's perspective, communicating their own perspective, merging differences and going to action, in all customer contacts, at a level that insures the customer is heard and feels served.

Skill Step #1: Get customer's perspective.

Repeat
Methods: Based on case study materials, trainees identify the customer's frame of reference and formulate responses.
Trainees repeat practice in getting perspective skills by working in triads.
- One trainee role plays the customer.
- One trainee assumes the role of the CSR.
- The third trainee evaluates the interaction.
- Roles are rotated after each interaction.

Example of Repeating

The *repeat* methods provide the trainees with the opportunity to exercise the skills. The trainees have the practice opportunity to insure skill acquisition. Now, develop at least one *repeat* method that you might employ to provide trainees with the opportunity to practice the skill.

OBJECTIVE: _____

Skill Step #1: _____
Repeat
Methods: _____

_____

_____

_____

_____

Practicing Repeating

Applying

Applying is still another way of doing. Applying is the ultimate purpose of the trainees acquiring the skills. Applying methods involve the uses or outcomes to which skills are put. They involve the generalizations or transfer of learning from the acquired skill to the applied skill. Most trainers are very uncomfortable with application methods because they have not been taught how to help trainees transfer their skill acquisition. After trainees have acquired and practiced the skills, they must learn the skill applications to take them back to the workplace. Trainees should be able to make more effective applications than they could prior to acquiring the new skills. For example, at some point in a company's history the need for electroplating skills was diagnosed, so a training program was designed to provide prospective employees with these skills. The test of effectiveness of the training is the trainees' application of the electroplating skills in the factory setting. The more effective the skill training, the more effective the trainees' skills application.

A very important requirement for developing application exercises is to be certain the trainees have already mastered all of the skills they will be expected to use within the application. Meeting this requirement insures success with the task of mastering the new skill. The trainees will have confidence in their performance, and thus are free to apply what is being trained. For example, when considering training supervisors how to do business writing, you might start by training them in the skills of writing a complete sentence. You could select writing a paragraph as an application, if the trainees have learned how to write a paragraph. Some *apply* methods that could be used for applications are writing memos, writing reports, writing letters and writing instructions. To practice the skills the trainees could write a paragraph (application) for a complaint letter (method) and then write a follow-up memo (method) using complete sentences (skill). As with repeat methods, *apply* methods can be varied by mixing procedures, e.g., case studies, contests, skits, role plays, worksheets with equipment and materials. Variety is also introduced by increasing the different types of situations in which trainees practice the skill.

Applying Methods

Providing trainees with opportunities to *apply* the skills in a real-life context is the next step in our sequence of teaching methods. *Application* methods insure the successful application of the skills. In implementing our delivery plan, our *application* methods address only the "exercise" step of content organization. In this respect *application* methods follow and duplicate the *repeat* methods during the exercise of the skills. For example, we can use *application* methods in implementing our presentation of the first skill step when training sales personnel in interpersonal communication skills.

PRESENTATION

OBJECTIVE: Customer Service Representatives (CSRs) will communicate interpersonally by getting the customer's perspective, communicating their own perspective, merging differences and going to action, in all customer contacts, at a level that insures the customer is heard and feels served.

Skill Step #1: Get customer's perspective.

Apply

Methods: Trainees are videotaped while role playing the following situations:
- A customer who wants the product.
- A customer who is very resistive to purchasing the product.
- An angry customer.
- A group of customers.

Trainees work in small groups to script a getting perspective interaction and videotape the interaction for the whole group.

Example of Applying

The *application* methods provide trainees with opportunities to use the skills in real-life contexts. The trainees are provided with the practical applications necessary to insure the utility of their skills application. Now, develop at least one *application* method you might employ to provide your trainees with the opportunity to apply a skill.

OBJECTIVE: _____

Skill Step #1: _____
Apply
Methods: _____

_____

_____

_____

_____

Practicing Applying

Exercises

We can apply the *tell-show-do* training methods in all areas of our lives and with any level of content detail. We can use them to train any new material while "thinking on our feet," in or out of the classroom. We can apply these training methods in any critical situation that involves training and learning. For example, we could employ *tell-show-do* methods for training in other work contexts.

OBJECTIVE: Trainers will train attending physically to security guards by using *tell-show-do* methods in formal security guard skills training at the highest level of attentiveness as measured by the defined attentiveness scale.

Training
Methods:
Tell: Teach "how to" steps.

Show: Model attending physically.

Do: Provide attending experience (sitting).

Repeat: Provide attending experience (standing).

Apply: Attend to others in real-life context.

Exercising Training Methods

Now try to develop training methods to achieve an important human resource development training skill objective:

OBJECTIVE: _____

_____

_____

Training
Methods:
Tell: _____

_____

Show: _____

_____

Do: _____

_____

Repeat: _____

_____

Apply: _____

_____

Repeat Exercise

Another example involves the training of receptionists to receive information.

> *OBJECTIVE:* The receptionist trainees will complete the appointment applicant screening by responding to content when interacting with applicants face-to-face or by telephone at an eighty percent level of accurate discrimination or better.

Training
Methods:

Tell: Describe the steps of responding to content as they relate to screening appointment applicants.

Show: Model directly and use videotaped demonstrations of successful use of responding to content when screening appointment applicants.

Do: Have receptionist trainees use the skills with each other and receive feedback.

Repeat: Have receptionist trainees use the skills with actors and receive feedback from the group.

Apply: Have the receptionist trainees use the skills on their jobs and receive feedback from their supervisors.

Exercising Training Methods

Now try to develop training methods to achieve an important information resource development training skill objective:

OBJECTIVE: _____

_____

_____

Training
Methods:
Tell: _____

_____

Show: _____

_____

Do: _____

_____

Repeat: _____

_____

Apply: _____

_____

Repeat Exercise

A third example involves *tell-show-do* methods for training machinists in gear cutting.

OBJECTIVE: The machinist trainee will cut four-inch helix gears using a milling machine with a hot rotary gear cutter and indexing mechanism at the specified tolerance specifications and within the specified time requirements.

Training
Methods:

Tell: Describe the machinery, gear blank and steps to be used to cut the four-inch helix gears.

Show: Demonstrate by actually doing each step involved in making the four-inch helix gears.

Do: Have the machinist, with direct supervision, complete each step as specified until the machinist has produced eight four-inch helix gears meeting the established tolerance specifications.

Repeat: Have the machinist complete, with sporadic, direct supervision, one hundred four-inch helix gears meeting the established tolerance specifications.

Apply: Have the machinist practice making the four-inch helix gears until the machinist has made one hundred in a row meeting established tolerance specifications within time requirements without direct supervision.

Exercising Training Methods

Now try to develop training methods to achieve an important technical training skill objective:

OBJECTIVE: _____

_____

_____

Training
Methods:
Tell: _____

_____

Show: _____

_____

Do: _____

_____

Repeat: _____

_____

Apply: _____

_____

Repeat Exercise

A final example shows *tell-show-do* methods for instructing trainees how to read resistors.

OBJECTIVE: The trainees will read the ohms ratings of ten different resistors during the training session with one hundred percent accuracy.

Training
Methods:

Tell: Describe how to read each of the resister bands and integrate the readings to get the total resistor value.

Show: Talk the trainees through the process of actually reading several resistors.

Do: Have trainees determine second resistor values under direct supervision.

Repeat: Have the trainees read the ohms ratings of ten different resistors while working in pairs, having one trainee read while the other checks the accuracy.

Apply: Have trainees identify and read the ohms rating of ten resistors on an assembled printed circuit board.

Exercising Training Methods

Now repeat developing training methods for another technical training skill objective:

OBJECTIVE: _____

_____

_____

Training
Methods:
Tell: _____

_____

Show: _____

_____

Do: _____

_____

Repeat: _____

_____

Apply: _____

_____

Repeat Exercise

You may wish to practice applying the development of training methods to your training specialty area. Try to make a variety of job-related applications. Also, try to make some applications to a home context or an educational context.

_____

_____

_____

_____

_____

Application Exercise

Summary

Perhaps you can now develop your training methods to achieve your skill objective in your training specialty. Simply outline how you would develop the training methods in achievable terms:

_____

_____

_____

_____

_____

If you are able to develop your training methods effectively, then we have accomplished our training skill objective:

The instructional trainees will develop training methods by employing various sensory modalities under formal and informal conditions with instructional trainees able to develop training methods to maximize trainee skill applications.

Indexing Training Methods

If you have accomplished our training skill objective, then you are capable of productively developing training methods to achieve your training skill objective in your specialty content:

TELL by Words
SHOW by Modeling
DO by Experiencing
REPEAT by Practicing
APPLY by Using

You will also be capable of "thinking on your feet" to develop training methods in any communications, formal or informal. You may also wish to involve your trainees in learning *tell-show-do* teaching methods in order to prepare them for communicating future contents to others.

TEACHING METHODS	CONTENT ORGANIZATION
Tell	Review • Overview • Present • Exercise • Summarize
Show	Review • Overview • Present • Exercise • Summarize
Do	Review • Overview • Present • Exercise • Summarize

Summarizing Training Methods

Expertise in our training methods is what publicly identifies us as trainers. The point of trainee involvement with both the trainers and the content is the training method which the trainer uses to deliver the content. The methods used to involve our trainees in the training reflect our own unique approaches to content delivery. We are "how" we train. There are as many different kinds of training as there are trainers, and our training methods reflect the uniqueness of our personal development. That is exhilarating! Unfortunately, not all trainers have effective training methods, even when individualized to their particular talents. The critical source of effectiveness is not the individualization of training methods to the trainer but the individualization of training methods to the trainees' talents. *Tell-Show-Do* training methods meet the trainees' hear-see-do needs for new skill acquisition. The trainees have their own opportunity to *tell-show-do* their learning during the repeat and apply stages of the exercise and summary steps of content organization. Thus, the trainees have the critical role in their own training. The trainees learn to be their own best trainers.

References

Bloom, B.S. *All Our Children Are Learning*. New York: McGraw-Hill, 1981.

Carkhuff, R.R. *The Development of Human Resources*. New York: Holt, Rinehart and Winston, 1971.

Carkhuff, R.R. *Toward Actualizing Human Potential*. Amherst, Mass.: Human Resource Development Press, 1981.

Carkhuff, R.R. and Berenson, D.H. *The Skilled Teacher*. Amherst, Mass.: Human Resource Development Press, 1981.

Dubin, R. and Taveggia, T.C. *The Teaching-Learning Paradox: A Comparative Analysis of College Teaching Methods*. Eugene, Ore.: Center for the Advanced Study of Educational Administration, University of Oregon, 1968.

Engel, H.M. *Handbook of Creative Learning Exercises*. Houston, Tex.: Gulf Publishing, 1973.

Gage, N.L. (Ed.). *The Psychology of Teaching Methods*. Chicago, Ill.: University of Chicago Press, 1976.

Gage, N.L. *The Scientific Basis of the Art of Teaching*. New York: Teachers College Press, 1977.

Howe, A. *International Yearbook of Education and Instructional Technology*. Chicago, Ill.: Nichols Publishing Co., 1980.

Kolb, D.A. *Learning Style Inventory*. Boston, Mass.: McBer and Co., 1976.

Laird, D. *Approaches to Training and Development*. Reading, Mass.: Addison-Wesley, 1982.

McKeachie, W.J. and Kulik, J.A. "Effective College Teaching." In F.N. Kerlinger (Ed.), *Review of Research on Education, Volume 3.* Itasca, Ill.: F.E. Peacock, 1975.

Nadler, L. *Designing Training Programs.* Reading, Mass.: Addison-Wesley, 1982.

Neidler, L.L. "Training Effectiveness: Changing Attitudes." *Training and Development Journal,* 1981, *35,* 24-28.

9

Developing the Training Delivery Plan

Trainees apply many of the skills acquired in training without ever thinking about them. Some remain unable to make skill applications in the work context. These trainees feel frustrated because they cannot perform the skills they should be prepared to do. Sometimes they never learned the skill in the first place—because trainers did not plan around the skill application. Planning involves determining the application to which the skills will be put and developing a plan to achieve that application. In other words, planning begins and ends with a skill application. The fundamental principle of a delivery plan states that all productive training deliveries are organized around a skill application. A delivery plan maximizes the conditions that facilitate learning the skill application. The delivery plan defines the objectives as well as develops and integrates content and training methods. Every phase of content organization interacts with every modality of training methods in emphasizing particular aspects of the skill content.

Review and Overview

In general, trainees learn best what they practice most (Berliner, 1977; Bloom, 1982; Gagne, 1977; Hultman, 1982; Killian, 1978). Thus, for example, if trainers emphasize making didactic presentations, trainees acquire the knowledge communicated. If trainers emphasize managing training exercises, trainees acquire skills and skill steps. In this context, trainees make the most skill applications in their work when the emphais is upon skill applications in their training (Bloom, 1982; Carkhuff and Berenson, 1981; Gagne, 1977; James, 1981). In other words, trainees must spend most of their training time involved in practical exercises emphasizing skill applications (American Education Research Association, 1966; Ausebel, 1978; Gage, 1976, 1977; Mager, 1966; McCullough, 1963; Mills, 1972). Delivery plans that emphasize combinations of methods and sequences that facilitate the trainees' movement toward the skill applications are most productive (Bloom, 1982; Gagne, 1977; Kaya, Gerhard, Staslewski and Berenson, 1967; Lefton and Buzzota, 1980; Rosenbaum, 1981). By employing the "variety principle," trainers can become most effective in bringing trainees into maximum contact with the training experience (Berenson, Berenson and Carkhuff, 1978; Bloom, 1981; Engel, 1973; Howe, 1980; James, 1981).

Principles of Delivery Plans

The training skill objective for this lesson is as follows:

The instructional trainees will develop delivery plans by integrating the content and methods under formal and informal conditions at a level insuring trainee skill applications.

Before you learn to develop your delivery plan, you may want an index of your skills in this area. Perhaps you can develop a delivery or lesson plan for some part of your training specialty. Simply outline how you would develop the delivery plan in achievable terms.

_____

_____

_____

_____

_____

Index Delivery Plans

You did well if you developed a delivery plan integrating the content organization with the training methods while emphasizing trainee skill applications. The effective factors emphasize integrating or crossing the sequences of organizing content with the training methods. We need all of these factors in combination with the skills and skill steps in order to insure our delivery and the trainees' acquisition of the skills. To this end, we will develop a ROPES by TELL-SHOW-DO delivery plan to facilitate the trainees' organization of the content.

CONTENT ORGANIZATION

	Review	Overview	Present	Exercise	Summarize
	Contingency Skills	Skill Applications	Skill Steps	Skill Steps	Skill Performance
TRAINING METHODS Tell					
Show					
Do					

Overviewing Delivery Plans

Defining Objectives

Before developing the training delivery plan we want to make a clear definition of the training skill objective. This will make it clear to all of the trainees what the purpose of the training experience is. We have had a good deal of experience in defining our training skill objectives. Again, the operations used to define the objectives include: components, functions, processes, conditions and standards. We may, in addition, add the key supportive knowledge necessary for the trainees.

OBJECTIVE: _____

_____

Components: Who and what?
Functions: What outcome?
Processes: How operates?
Conditions: Where and when?
Standards: How well?

Reviewing Objectives

Here is our example of the training skill objective for training sales personnel to communicate with the customer:

OBJECTIVE: Customer Service Representatives (CSRs) will communicate interpersonally by getting the customer's perspective, communicating their own perspective, merging differences and going to action, in all customer contacts, at a level that insures the customer is heard and feels served.

This sample training skill objective becomes the first component of the training delivery plan.

Example of a Training Skill Objective

In preparation of developing a training plan, you may find it helpful to once again define a training skill objective in your specialty content.

OBJECTIVE: _____

_____

_____

_____

_____

Practicing Training Skill Objectives

Developing Content

We will also want to develop an outline of the skills content before developing our training delivery plan. An outline of the skills content tells the trainers where they are going and also how to get there. Again, we have had a great deal of experience in developing our skills content. We utilize our *do* and *think* steps to define the skill steps to achieve the training skill objective.

OBJECTIVE: _____

_____

DO Steps: Major actions

DO Substeps: Minor actions

Reviewing Content Development

Here is our example of the interpersonal communication skills content for sales personnel. This content outline will be used when developing our training delivery plan.

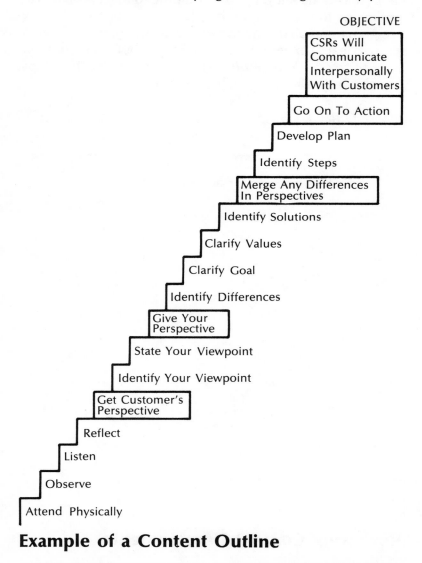

Example of a Content Outline

Again, you might find it helpful to outline the skills content in your training specialty.

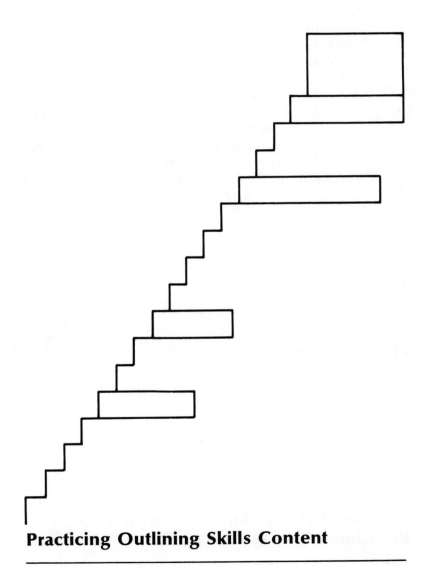

Practicing Outlining Skills Content

Finally we will want to develop *think* steps and the *supportive knowledge* for each skill step or substep.

Think Steps:
    Before: Resources?
    During: Corrections?
    After: Performance?

Supportive Knowledge:
    Facts: Names of components, functions and processes.
    Concepts: Relationships among components, functions and processes.
    Principles: Implications of facts and concepts.

Reviewing Think Steps and Supportive Knowledge

Here is an example of the *think* steps and *supportive knowledge* for the first skill step, getting the customer's perspective, for our interpersonal communication objective.

Think Steps:
- **Before:** Is the setting appropriate?
  Is the time appropriate?
- **During:** Am I attending correctly?
  Am I observing facial expressions and body posture?
  Am I listening to content and voice tone?
  Am I reflecting feeling and content?
- **After:** Did I accurately capture the customer's viewpoint?
  Did I reflect in a way the customer could accept?
  Did I sound genuine?

Supportive Knowledge:
- **Facts:** Attending physically, observing, listening, reflecting, genuineness.
- **Concepts:** If the salesperson gets the customer's perspective, then she (or he) will understand the customer.
- **Principles:** If the salesperson gets the customer's perspective, then she (or he) will understand the customer so that the salesperson will have the information needed to serve or persuade the customer.

Example of Think Steps and Supportive Knowledge

You may find it helpful to practice developing the details of your content before developing your training delivery plan.

Skill Step: _____

Think Steps:
Before: _____

_____

During: _____

_____

After: _____

_____

Supportive Knowledge:
Facts: _____

_____

Concepts: _____

_____

Principles: _____

_____

Practicing Think Steps and Supportive Knowledge

Developing Delivery Plans

Now we are ready to develop our training delivery plan. The delivery plan will guide us in making our training delivery. The delivery plan can be developed for any level of content detail, e.g., training skill objective, skill step or skill substep. We organize our content and methods in a way that enables us to know when to perform training skills and when to manage trainee skill performance. A *show* step for interpersonal and performance appraisal skills and formats for *doing, repeating,* and *applying* your delivery plan skills in different aspects of your training specialty follow on succeeding pages. Select your own training methods within the *tell-show-do* methods. Try to vary the applications in your training specialty in order to fully benefit from the practice.

REVIEWING: *Tell - Show - Do* Contingency Skills
OVERVIEWING: *Tell - Show - Do* Skill Applications
PRESENTING: *Tell - Show - Do* Skill Steps
EXERCISING: *Tell - Show - Do* Skill Steps
SUMMARIZING: *Tell - Show - Do* Skill Performance

Developing Delivery Plans

IMPLEMENTING A RESULTS-ORIENTED PERFORMANCE APPRAISAL SYSTEM CONTENT ORGANIZATION

TRAINING METHODS	REVIEW	OVERVIEW	PRESENT	EXERCISE	SUMMARIZE
TELL	• Supervisors discuss positive and negative experiences with performance appraisal (PA).	• Trainer plays videotape of chief executive officer detailing functions of PA in company.	• Trainer lectures on each step of completing a PA form (result areas, measures, standards). • Trainer lectures on each step of required communication skills (getting perspective, giving perspective, merging differences).	• Supervisors develop a model for linking PA steps and interpersonal communication steps.	• Supervisors develop a one page reminder for how to do PA.
SHOW	• Review examples of different PA forms and discuss function.	• Trainer plays videotape of a supervisor and employee working together to develop a PA plan.	• Trainer uses overhead of PA form to show each PA step. • Trainer shows video of supervisor and employee, pointing out each skill step.	• Trainer demonstrates using PA planning skills with interpersonal skills.	• Supervisors develop a model completed PA form for each occupation they supervise.
DO	• Supervisors write standards, based on case study material. Discuss implications of results.	• Supervisors work in small groups to brainstorm possible barriers to PA. Barriers are presented to whole group and possible solutions are discussed.	• Supervisors complete a PA form, step by step, using case material. • Supervisors practice each step of interpersonal communications by role playing in a "goldfish bowl" context.	• Supervisors complete a PA form for one of their employees. • Supervisors role play interpersonal skills in triads. • Supervisors role play completing a PA form with an employee on videotape.	• Based on case study materials, supervisors complete a PA form and review it with an employee in a simulated office situation.

Sample Delivery Plan

SKILLS CONTENT ORGANIZATION

TRAINING METHODS	REVIEW	OVERVIEW	PRESENT	EXERCISE	SUMMARIZE
TELL					
SHOW					
DO					

Delivery Plan Repeat Exercise

ORIENTATION TO EMPLOYEE BENEFITS CONTENT ORGANIZATION

TRAINING METHODS	REVIEW	OVERVIEW	PRESENT	EXERCISE	SUMMARIZE
TELL	Entry Training Experience Example: • Trainees discuss what constitutes compensation for job.	• Trainer lectures briefly on each major benefit program: — Major Medical — Dental — Life Insurance	• Trainees lectures on each program in detail, referring to appropriate section of employee benefits information package.	• Trainees ask any final questions.	• Trainees describe benefits they will receive.
SHOW	• Trainees build a list of past compensation they have received.	• Trainer gives example of benefits that have been paid out to employees.	• Trainer gives examples of benefits provided under different coverages.	• Trainees show draft of completed forms to trainer.	• Trainees illustrate how coverage selected will meet their needs.
DO	• Trainees categorize compensation into monetary and non-monetary.	• Trainees tentatively list coverage they want.	• Trainees select coverage they want. Group fills out forms together, based on case material.	• Trainees complete final forms.	• Trainer uses a true/false test to evaluate trainee understanding of benefits.

Sample Delivery Plan

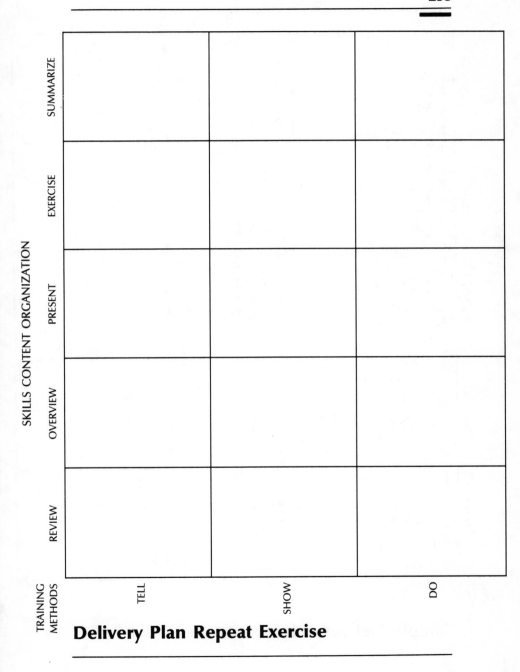

Delivery Plan Repeat Exercise

Sample Delivery Plan

COMPUTER WIRE SOLDERING CONTENT ORGANIZATION

TRAINING METHODS	REVIEW	OVERVIEW	PRESENT	EXERCISE	SUMMARIZE
TELL	Entry Training Experience Example: • Trainees describe all the tools needed for soldering and their use.	• Use lecture and handouts to describe what the soldering task is, its function in the computer assembly process, how it is done, and that without these connections, the computer won't work.	• Describe preparing the materials, mechanical joining, soldering the connection and inspecting the connection.	• Have trainees describe successes and mistakes in the process.	• Have trainees describe soldering process learned.
SHOW	• Trainer illustrates the use of the tools needed for soldering.	• Show trainees the connections and their operations.	• Have trainees watch the actual soldering process as demonstrated by the trainer.	• Have trainees illustrate proper techniques to avoid mistakes for each other.	• Have trainees illustrate proper techniques.
DO	• Have each trainee use the tools to solder and assess their competency.	• Have them physically examine the assembled computer and the connections.	• Have trainees practice soldering with supervision.	• Have trainees practice until they can do 50 soldered connections in a row without mistake.	• Have each trainee complete soldered connections within a specified amount of time, and assess number and quality.

SKILLS CONTENT ORGANIZATION

	REVIEW	OVERVIEW	PRESENT	EXERCISE	SUMMARIZE
TELL					
SHOW					
DO					

TRAINING METHODS

Delivery Plan Repeat Exercise

You may have realized that your delivery plan was your skill application for Book 1. You participated in training modules that incorporated all of the ingredients of preparing content: defining the skill objective; developing the skill steps and supportive knowledge; organizing the content and training methods. Now you have performed *do, repeat* and *apply* steps in your training specialty. You now know how to develop delivery plans in your training specialty. You may also develop different delivery plans for different work, training and home applications, such as the different skill applications you addressed in each skill area. Put succinctly, the delivery plan enables you to make a productive skill delivery of any skill in any area of human endeavor.

SKILL APPLICATIONS
Work
Training
Home

Applying Delivery Plans

Summary
Perhaps you can now develop your delivery plan for your training specialty. Outline how you would develop the delivery plan in achievable terms.

_____

_____

_____

_____

    If you are able to develop your delivery plan effectively, then we have accomplished our training skill objective:

> _The instructional trainees will develop delivery plans by integrating the content and methods under formal and informal conditions at a level insuring trainee skill applications._

Indexing Delivery Plans

If you have accomplished our training skill objective, then you are capable of productively developing your delivery plans to deliver your skill objectives in your training specialty. You will also be capable of "thinking on your feet" to develop delivery plans in any training content. You may also wish to involve your trainees in developing their roles in the implementation of delivery plans in order to prepare them to achieve skill objectives in their lives.

CONTENT ORGANIZATION

	Review	Overview	Present	Exercise	Summarize
TRAINING METHODS					
Tell	CS	SA	SS	SS	SP
Show	CS	SA	SS	SS	SP
Do	CS	SA	SS	SS	SP

KEY

CS — Contingency Skills
SA — Skill Applications
SS — Skill Steps
SP — Skill Performance

Summarizing Delivery Plans

The generic training methods used in conjunction with the steps of content organization parallel our trainees' involvement in the learning process. Reviewing the content involves using *tell-show-do* training methods to diagnose the contingency skills. Then the trainees will know what they can and cannot do. The trainees can explore where they are in relation to the new training tasks. Overviewing the content involves using *tell-show-do* training methods to illustrate the potential skill applications. Then the trainees will know when to use the skill. They can understand where they are in relation to where they want to be with the training tasks. Presenting the content involves using *tell-show-do* training methods to train the skill steps. Then the trainees will know how to do the skills. They can act to get from where they are to where they want to be with the training tasks.

Exercising the content involves using *repeat* and *apply* training methods as well as *tell-show-do* training methods to practice the skill, and reinforces the trainees' acting to achieve their goals. Summarizing the content involves using *tell-show-do* training methods to provide the trainees with an opportunity to demonstrate what they have learned. Thus, the trainees have another chance to experientially engage the skills. They can complete their acting to achieve their training goals.

References

American Education Research Association. *Review of Educational Research.* Washington, D.C.: American Education Research Association, 1966.

Ausebel, D.P. *Educational Psychology.* New York: Holt, Rinehart and Winston, 1978.

Berenson, S.R., Berenson, D.H. and Carkhuff, R.R. *The Skills of Teaching—Lesson Planning Skills.* Amherst, Mass.: Human Resource Development Press, 1978.

Berliner, D.C. *Instructional Time in Research on Teaching.* San Francisco, Calif.: Far West Laboratory for Educational Research and Development, 1977.

Bloom, B. *All Our Children Are Learning.* New York: McGraw-Hill, 1981.

Bloom, B. *Human Characteristics and School Learning.* New York: McGraw-Hill, 1982.

Carkhuff, R.R. and Berenson, D.H. *The Skilled Teacher.* Amherst, Mass.: Human Resource Development Press, 1981.

Engel, H.M. *Handbook of Creative Learning Exercises.* Houston, Tex.: Gulf Publishing, 1973.

Gage, N.L. (Ed.). *The Psychology of Teaching Methods.* Chicago, Ill.: University of Chicago Press, 1976.

Gage, N.L. *The Scientific Basic of the Art of Teaching.* New York: Teachers College Press, 1977.

Gagne, R.M. *Conditions of Learning.* New York: Holt, Rinehart and Winston, 1977.

Howe, A. *International Yearbook of Education and Instructional Technology.* Chicago, Ill.: Nichols Publishing Co., 1980.

Hultman, K.E. "The Key to Whiz Bang Training." *Training,* 1982, *19,* 33-34.

James, R. "Training, Learning and the Instructor's Role." *Human Resource Development*, 1981, *5*, 17-20.

Kaya, E., Gerhard, M., Staslewski, A. and Berenson, D.H. *Developing a Theory of Educational Practices at the Elementary School.* Norwalk, Conn.: Ford Foundation Fund for the Improvement of Education, 1967.

Killian, R.A. "Developing Full Performance and Potential." Chapter in *Human Resource Development.* Chicago, Ill.: American Management Association, 1978.

Lefton, R.E. and Buzzota, V.R. "Trainers, Learners and Training Results." *Training and Development Journal*, 1980, *34*, 12-14.

Mager, R.F. and Beach, K.M. *Developing Vocational Instruction.* San Francisco, Calif.: Fearon Publishers, 1966.

McCullough, C.M. "What Does Research Reveal About Practices in Teaching Reading?" In N.L. Gage (Ed.), *Handbook of Research on Teaching.* Chicago, Ill.: Rand McNally, 1963.

Mills, H.R. *Teaching and Training.* New York: Halstead Press, 1972.

Rosenbaum, B.L. "Modeling Versus Motivation." *Industrial Marketing*, 1981, *70*, 76.

SUMMARY AND TRANSITION

Training does not stand in isolation from other experiences, both antecedent and consequential. Its trainers as well as trainees have as the source of their development their own education and experience. In turn, training has as its consequences the human resource development that, in interaction with information resource development, accounts for "working smarter" and improving productivity.

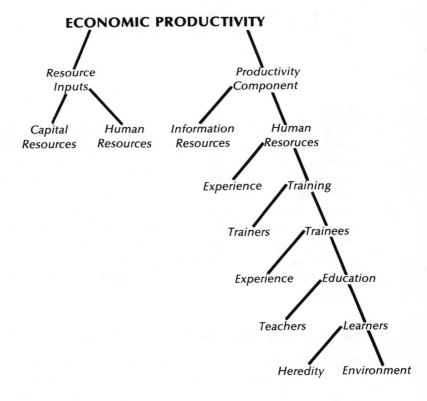

ECONOMIC PRODUCTIVITY

10

Sources of Training Effectiveness

Much has been written yet little is understood about the sources of effect in training. In this context, it is helpful to see training in terms of its likely historical antecedents as well as its potential future consequences. In other words, we must look at any given group of trainees in terms of the sources of their development as well as the effects on their development as a consequence of training. We may view the trainees in terms of propositions organizing their antecedents and consequences. We may also derive corollaries from these fundamental propositions.

Sources of Trainee Development

Because the trainees are, themselves, products of a series of experiences, it is helpful to view them in terms of their origins. Thus trainees, originally learners, are products of certain kinds of learning factors.

1. *The learner is a product of hereditary and environmental factors.*

Every argument that can be marshalled for either heredity or environment can be marshalled for the other. Clearly, the amount of variance accounted for by either of these factors depends upon the potency of the factor.

a. *The hereditary factor emphasizes physical and intellectual development.* With the nervous system as the basis for intelligence, human functionality is at its core physical and therefore hereditary.

b. *The environmental factor emphasizes the processes that impact the hereditary factor.* Primarily family processes impact hereditary factors to facilitate or retard intellectual development (Coleman, 1966).

2. *Education is a function of learner and teacher factors.*

Productive education culminating in learner achievement is a function of both learner and teacher factors. Where teachers are not potent, learner variables dominate (Gage, 1977). Where teachers are potent, both teacher and learner variables contribute to learner achievement (Carkhuff and Berenson, 1981; Carkhuff, Fisher, Cannon, Friel and Pierce, 1984).

a. *Learner variables emphasize pre-instructional variables.* Learner pre-instructional performance is the best predictor of post-instructional performance (Gage, 1977).

b. *Teacher variables emphasize teacher skills.* Teacher skills include specialty content and teaching delivery skills (Carkhuff and Berenson, 1981; Carkhuff, Fisher, Cannon, Friel and Pierce, 1984).

3. *Trainees are a product of education and experience factors.*
   The robustness of the contributions of these factors depends upon the processing skills acquired in education; that is, the higher the quality of processing skills acquired through education the more robust the education and experience factors (Carkhuff, Fisher, Cannon, Friel and Pierce, 1984).
   a. *Education factors emphasize the learners' specialty content and processing skills.* The trainees' contribution depends upon their level of expertise in content and their ability to learn new content.
   b. *Experience factors emphasize the quantity of experience in a specialty area.* Whereas the education factors emphasize processing for the quality of experience, the experience factors emphasize the quantity of experience or time in a specialty area.
4. *Training is a function of trainee and trainer factors.*
   Productive training culminating in trainee skills gain is a function of both trainee and trainer factors (Carkhuff, 1969; Carkhuff, Fisher, Cannon, Friel and Pierce, 1984). In general, trainees move toward the trainers' levels of functioning in a specialty area.
   a. *Trainee factors emphasize the trainees' specialty content, processing skills and experiential applications.* The trainees' contributions are a function of their ability to apply their learning to their experience.
   b. *Trainer factors emphasize training skills.* Training skills include instructional design and training delivery skills (Carkhuff, Fisher, Cannon, Friel and Pierce, 1984; Carkhuff and Berenson, 1981).
5. *Individual human resource development is a function of training and experience factors.*

Human resource development is a function of the quality of the training and the quantity of experience. High quality training interacts to increase the contributions of experience (Carnavale, 1983; Denison, 1979; Grayson, 1980; Kendrick, 1979).

  a. *Training factors emphasize the trainees' specialty content and processing skills.* The growing level of expertise in the specialty content and the trainees' ability to learn new content are key factors in training.

  b. *Experience factors emphasize the quantity of experience in a specialty area.* The quality of training derives the contribution of experience to human resource development.

6. *Organizational productivity is a function of human and information resource development.*
These factors may be seen in interaction with each other in "working smarter" (Carnavale, 1983; Denison, 1979; Grayson, 1980; Kendrick, 1979). Human resources produce advancements in knowledge which, in turn, produce more highly developed human resources.

  a. *Human resource development emphasizes human processing.* Human processing emphasizes analyzing, operationalizing and technologizing information to develop human and information resources.

  b. *Information resource development emphasizes information processing.* Information processing emphasizes analyzing, synthesizing and projecting data to develop human and information resources.

7. *Economic productivity is a function of productivity and input factors.*
Economic productivity is largely a function of

increasing productivity. It is also a function of reducing input factors (Carnavale, 1983; Denison, 1979; Grayson, 1980; Kendrick, 1979).

a. *Productivity factors emphasize human and information resource development.* The quality of personnel interacts productively with advancements in knowledge.

b. *Input factors emphasize human and capital resource factors.* The input factors required are two-thirds personnel and one-third capital.

To sum, training is best viewed in terms of its historical antecedents as well as its potential consequences. The sources of effect of training depend upon the potency of the trainers. Where trainers are high level functioning exemplary performers with instructional design and training delivery skills, they are potent sources of effect in training. Where trainers are neither exemplars nor skilled in training skills, the trainees themselves will be the dominant sources of effect (Carkhuff, 1969; Carkhuff and Berenson, 1981).

The trainees move part of the way toward a high level functioning trainer. In our own research on teaching and training (Carkhuff, 1969), we have found trainee achievement to be a function of the discrepancy in functioning between trainer and trainees in the relevant dimension. In general, the trainee achieves approximately one-half the discrepancy in functioning between trainer and trainee. Specifically, the formula for the effects of training upon trainee functioning is as follows:

$$\text{Trainee Gain} = \tfrac{1}{2}\,\text{Trainer's Functioning} - \tfrac{1}{2}\,\text{Trainees' Functioning} + \tfrac{1}{20}\,\text{Discrepancy} + 0.2\,\text{Constant}$$

Of course, the trainers themselves are products of their own education and experience. Their skills in content and delivery will be a function of the interaction of the quality of their education with their experience in training.

In turn, one of the products of training is the development of human resources. Human resources interact with individual resources to account for the productivity component. The productivity component and resource inputs are the primary sources of economic productivity.

Thus, training plays a central role in improving economic productivity through human and information resource development. In turn, the trainee, depending upon training skills, is a critical source of effect in training effectiveness. Trainee improvement in functioning on any dimension is a function of the trainers' skills: skills in preparing and making a training delivery. In Volume I, we have learned the skills involved in preparing the training delivery. Now in Volume II, we will learn the skills involved in making a training delivery.

References

Carkhuff, R.R. *Helping and Human Relations.* New York: Holt, Rinehart and Winston, 1969.

Carkhuff, R.R. and Berenson, D.H. *The Skilled Teacher.* Amherst, Mass.: Human Resource Development Press, 1981.

Carkhuff, R.R., Fisher, S.G., Cannon, J.R., Friel, T.W. and Pierce, R.M. *Instructional Systems Design, Volumes I and II.* Amherst, Mass.: Human Resource Development Press, 1984.

Carnavale, A. *Human Capital.* Washington, D.C.: American Society for Training and Development, 1983.

Coleman, J.S. *Equality of Educational Opportunity.* Washington, D.C.: U.S. Government Printing Office, 1966.

Denison, E. *Accounting for Slower Economic Growth.* Washington, D.C.: Brookings Institution, 1979.

Gage, N.L. *The Scientific Basis of the Art of Teaching.* New York: Teachers College Press, 1977.

Grayson, C.J. *The U.S. Economy and Productivity.* Washington, D.C.: Joint Economic Committee, 1980.

Kendrick, J. *Productivity Trends and the Recent Slowdown.* Washington, D.C.: American Enterprise Institute, 1979.

INDEX

C

D